ANDREA ROBINSON'S

2011 WINE BUYING GUIDE

ANDREA'S "TOP TEN" WINES

for Everyone

PUBLISHED BY JGR PRODUCTIONS, INC.

www.Andreawine.com

First edition published 2002

Previously published in the United States by Broadway Books, an imprint of The Doubleday Broadway Publishing Group, a division of Random House, Inc., New York

The Library of Congress has cataloged the first edition as follows:
Immer, Andrea
[Wine buying guide for everyone]
Andrea Immer's wine buying guide for everyone /
Andrea Immer; edited by Anthony Giglio.—1st ed.
p. cm.
Includes index.
1. Wine and wine making. I. Title: Wine buying guide
for everyone. II. Giglio, Anthony. III. Title.

TP548 .I4624 2002
641.2'2—dc21   2002023077

ISBN-13: 978-0-9771032-6-3
ISBN-10: 0-9771032-6-9

PRINTED IN THE UNITED STATES OF AMERICA

10 9 8 7 6 5 4 3 2 1

CONTENTS

INTRODUCTION

Welcome to my completely new *Wine Buying Guide for Everyone* After eight editions, I am excited to debut a brand-new format that will make it even easier for you to find and enjoy great wines without spending a fortune. While I have always focused this guide on wines with good availability and great quality for the price, I am now taking that concept to a whole new level, including only wines that have ranked in my Top Ten in their category **balancing quality and price**, and focusing on what I call FAVE wines.

Top Ten Wines

Every wine in this Guide is one of my Top Ten picks in its category. To put it simply, you don't have to worry about a wine's score, because every wine in this guide is a winner. Because all the wines are great, I even thought about eliminating the scores but decided to keep them in, at least for now (more on that later).

Another benefit to allowing only 10 wines per major category is that I have simplified your shopping challenge. For example, I think loading you up with over 40 brands that could reasonably be in anyone's list of great California Chardonnays under $25 just isn't helpful enough. For categories like this one, getting the list down to 10 was hard work (ha!) but hey, someone has to do it! So again, if it's in this book, its great juice.

Featuring only the Top Ten wines in each category also allowed me to create a guide that can cover the world of wine within the pages of a reasonably sized pocket book or, if you're online, or on your handheld device or iPad, you can see my favorites across all the major categories within a manageable number of search parameters.

FAVE Wines

So what is a FAVE wine? Well, a FAVE wine is:

Food-friendly - Wine was meant for food! So my first requirement for FAVE wines is to be Food-friendly. That means wines that are relatively higher in acidity and lower in oak and alcohol, because crisp acidity accents food flavors, and lower oak and alcohol lets the flavors in both the wine and the food shine. Having said that, some of the most noted critics give high scores to wines that, while impressive at first sip, are too "big" from oak and alcohol and too low in acidity to go well with many foods.

Authentic - A FAVE wine must also be authentic to its grape and place. A Barolo from Italy should taste like a Barolo from Italy. How else could you know what to expect based on the label? And if you are preparing a dish to go with Barolo, you don't want to open a Zinfandel in disguise. This is another problem with "big" wines - their heavy oak and alcohol often mask the unique attributes that I look for in a wine from a particular region.

For wine lovers, the authenticity of grape and place in wines is exciting, because it ensures great diversity of flavors, scents, and styles and therefore, always something new to discover. Wine geeks refer to this as "terroir" - the unique expression of a particular vineyard region, varietal and vintner. To be Authentic, a wine must be true to its terroir.

Note: to be Authentic, some wines *should* be "big." In other words the terroir simply *creates* a big wine. For example, red wines from the Priorat region of Spain are going to be big, but since they come by that style naturally, the best wines from Priorat are balanced and still go well with food. Granted, they are best with big food but hey, sometimes a hearty meal really hits the spot. Try a great Priorat with smoked tri-tip and you will see what I mean.

Value - You can find Value at any price. A wine that costs less than $15 can be truly extraordinary. I prefer many of these wines to the pricier ones. Lower-priced wines with extraordinary quality are the Value gems and I focus a lot on these in the guide.

So why pay more? Well, there are expensive wines that also offer great Value (especially if someone else is paying!). Obviously, the higher the price the more extraordinary the wine needs to be to deliver Value. The expensive wines in this book are truly amazing.

Extraordinary wine - And on that note, a FAVE wine must be Extraordinary. These wines will impress even the most discerning palates. While the Value criterion allows me to assess a wine relative to its price, the "Extraordinary" requirement allows me to rate the wine's absolute level of quality.

So, wouldn't *every* credible critic be looking for FAVE wines? The answer is no and that's just fine because every palate is different, even amongst the "experts."

And the fact is that some of the top critics often overlook many of the most outstanding FAVE-style bottlings because the wines are too subtle and nuanced to stand out in a tasting with bigger wines (see sidebar). That does not mean their ratings are *wrong*, just different from mine - because they have different tastes, and a different approach (more on mine below).

So how do you find an expert whose palate is like yours? All you have to do is try some of their picks and see if you agree or not. That's right, you can dis-agree with an "expert" and be right. Remember, it is *your* palate. You know what you like. Over time, you will find a critic whose preferred style of wine is simi-lar to yours (hopefully that's me!). Since critics taste so many wines, they can really help you wade through all the choices and find wines *you* will love.

WHY "BIG" WINES SCORE BIG: It actually makes sense that many critics would give big wines big scores, and I will tell you why. As I and other wine pros know from experience, when you taste a large number of wines at one sitting, often without food, the wines with high alcohol and oak, and lower acidity, stand out to a fatigued palate. Wines with higher acidity and more subtlety or earthiness get clobbered, or taste thin by comparison - especially without the food for which they were meant! **So, "big wines" often get the big scores.**

Wine Scores
The Facts (and fiction) about Wine Scores

OK, so even the experts' palates are different and you alone can determine which wines you like. But since you don't taste through as many wines as the experts, finding a critic whose palate pleases yours is useful. But how much weight should you put on the specific scores they give the wines?

Well, many of my friends in the industry, especially winemakers, believe that when critics put a specific score on a wine it creates a lot of problems. They contend that consumers put too much weight on the scores and not enough weight on their own opinions and/or the uniqueness of the wine. There is a famous cartoon in which a customer in a wine shop tells the merchant that he does not like a particular wine, and the merchant responds by telling the customer that the wine got a "98" from a well-known critic. The consumer then says, "OK, I'll take a case!"

The financial impact of wine scores is undeniable and the impact on styles of winemaking has also been dramatic. Since the important scores come from only a few key critics, consultants have emerged to help winemakers make wines to please those critics. Needless to say, this economic reality can impair the winemakers' ability to make the wine based on the authentic expression of the grapes, the place and/or their own particular style.

I hope that this guide, the growing access to a wider variety of critics' (and consumer) input, and increased consumer confidence in their own palate, will reduce this unfortunate effect of wine scores.

Another criticism of putting specific scores on wines is that no critic, no matter how skilled, can be consistent with their ratings. Critics of wine scores also believe that a specific score creates a false level of accuracy.

Although I agree with these points at some level, I am confident that I can be consistent within a few points each time I taste a wine. I believe the key for accurate, consistent and fair tastings is to always taste wines as follows:

1. All wines are tasted "blind" i.e., without knowing the wine's identity.
2. The wines are tasted with fair competition i.e., the same grape, region, and price range.
3. A "Benchmark" wine is included in the tasting i.e., a wine that I know is consistently tops in the category.
4. The number of wines tasted at one sitting is limited to maintain sharpness (even spitting has its limits).
5. The wines are always tasted with food even if it is just an appropriate cheese.

Even with this approach, bottle variation and other factors can move a wine's score a few points in either direction *but*, there is no question that the difference between an 87 and 89 is minor. Having said that, the score is unlikely to change more than 3 or 4 points in either direction, so if you don't over-analyze the score but instead put it in the context of the place, grape and price, you can be confident that a high- scoring wine is a high-quality wine.

Having said that, I've kept my scores in because I know from experience that if I am going to help people find great wines, they need to know my bottom line and the bottom line that consumers understand best is a score. Providing you with a score also allows me to communicate my opinion of the relative quality from wine to wine. The tasting notes are there to help further your appreciation of each wine's unique attributes, and the pairing notes will help you make the most of every bottle with a great food match.

I also think that since my FAVE approach is so different from some of the other popular critics, getting my score out there can help create a balance of opinions and support a greater diversity of wine styles. (I hope you'll weigh in on andreawine.com with any feedback!)

So now you know the truth: a high score from a critic doesn't necessarily mean that you will or even should love the wine. And a very high score almost certainly guarantees that the wine will be hard to find and expensive. That makes wine shopping strictly by the numbers a hassle, and a big gamble if your palate and the critic's aren't on the same wavelength. It is partly for this reason that with a few exceptions, the wines in this guide are broadly available. Putting scores on broadly available wines is unlikely to significantly change their price.

I want to be clear that I am not saying you should avoid high-scoring wines. The leading critics have lots of tasting experience and know quality in wine, so many of their top-scoring bottles are indeed great and worth trying if you can find and afford them or get the chance to try them on someone else's nickel. (Most of the time that's the only the way we sommeliers can afford to try them!).

My mantras:

1. *It doesn't have to be expensive to be good.* I've preached this gospel for a long time, and I think the message is really catching on now. While it is true that you can pay more and get a better wine, it is also true that a higher price doesn't guarantee the wine will be better, or that *you* will like it more. Obviously, pricey wines should really deliver, but I also hold my lower priced value wines to an "Extraordinary" high standard. They are the intro to wine for most people, and you know what they say about first impressions!

2. *Your palate is all that matters.* If you like a wine, then by definition it is a quality wine for you. So don't fret if your favorite wine is not included in this guide. In fact, go to my website and let me know, I never mind trying new wines. A lot of great wines do not make this book simply because the wine's availability isn't sufficiently broad or, I have found other wines in the same category that I think are better.

3. *Quality comes from the vineyard.* As any pro will tell you, it takes great grapes to make great wine,

and where each type of grape is planted (soil, sun, slope, etc.) is critical to its ultimate quality potential. In other words, Chardonnay in an average vineyard site will taste like average white wine, while Chardonnay in an ideally-suited site can taste sublime. As such, the best vineyards command top prices for their grape crops, and that drives up the price of the wines made from them. So, often there is an important connection between quality and price.

Final thoughts...

In addition to limiting my picks to 10 wines per category and focusing on FAVE wines, I have applied the following thinking to what goes into this guide:

1. Consistency - Although the guide is published every year and vintage does matter, the wines in this book have demonstrated a consistent quality that allows this guide to be used for wines that don't match the vintage in this edition. Obviously, it is best to find the specific notes and scores for the specific vintage, but in general, you are safe going with these wines within a year or two of the specified vintage.

2. Value bias - In choosing what brands to include, I focus above all on *taste*, with a heavy bias toward *quality for the price*, and *track record* (quality consistency). Why? There are literally thousands of wines on the market; and even the 100 or so labels in a warehouse store, or the 30 bottles on a casual restaurant wine list, can seem overwhelming.

3. Availability - There is nothing more frustrating for wine lovers than to read about a great wine and then be unable to find it. For this reason, the vast majority of wines in this guide are broadly available.

4. Discoveries *I also spotlight an exciting array of "new kids on the block" that show real promise.* The constant emergence of new talent, whether in music, sports, or wine, is part of the fun. As much as sommeliers love to praise the prowess of the longtime leaders in wine quality, we also love to turn our guests (and readers) on to new discoveries. This book includes those I've found in the last year or so that are really worth seeking out.

My Scores and Reviews

Each wine entry includes my tasting notes and score for the wine. In addition, if I have discovered a great-tasting dish or cheese to pair with the wine, I share it.

I keep the rating criteria simple, with taste scores listed on a 100-point scale, a well-established industry standard. Here is how the scores are defined:

0–69 Poor (not included)

70-79 Fair (not included)

80-85 Good (not included)

86-89 **Very good** - A very good-quality, well-made wine that is very pleasant to drink

90-94 ***Excellent*** - A wine that is wonderful to drink, and is exemplary in its category and the world of wine

95-100 ***Amazing*** - A wine that rocks your world and seizes your senses with its utterly exciting complexity and expressiveness.

Note that for this buying guide, I only include wines rated as very good, excellent or amazing. With limited space in this book and time on your hands, I prefer to use it telling you what you *should* buy, rather than what to avoid.

Kitchen Survivor™ Grades

"How long will a wine keep after it's opened?" Having heard this question more than any other from my restaurant customers and wine students, I decided several years ago to start putting wines to the "kitchen survivor test." The resulting report card should help you make the most of the leftovers, by simply recorking and storing them in the fridge or on the counter, for enjoying later. Refer to How the Guide is Organized for a breakdown of how the grading works.

Your Notes

There's space in each listing for your notes so you can keep track of the wines you try, and you can also enter your ratings and reviews at my Web site, Andreawine. com. Set up a free profile, and then you can search by wine name, and add your review.

Other Helpful Tools In the Guide

Throughout the *Guide,* I've included simple tools to address just about every major wine buying question I've ever been asked. They are:

High-Flying Wines—I now choose the wines for Delta Air Lines Business Elite®. Check out pages 160-165 to learn more about our "cellar in the sky"!

Food & Wine Pairing Basics—The core techniques sommeliers use to expertly match wine and food.

Affordable Agers—My short-list of wines that will age well for ten years or longer in your cellar, while not costing an arm and a leg. Cheers to that!

Entertaining with Wine—Everyone loves a wine party, and serving the right wine can make even a casual gathering memorable. These are my tips on choosing, buying the right amount, serving and highlighting wine when you're having company.

Wine List Decoder—This handy cross-reference chart will help you crack the code of wine list terms, so you can quickly and easily find the styles you like.

Andrea's Complete Wine Course "Mini-Course"—Mini-lessons covering wine styles, label terms, glassware, buying wine in stores and restaurants, and other housekeeping details to simplify buying and serving wine, so you can focus on enjoying it

And finally, with so many guides out there, why keep publishing this one? Well, I believe that by focusing on Food Friendliness, Authentic wines, and Value, this guide really fills a gap. Most people around the country buy wine based on price and convenience. And whether it's my wine students, TV viewers, or visitors to my Web site, www.andreawine.com, they all have the same questions: What are the good, inexpensive wines? And if I'm going to splurge, which wines are really worth it? This is the only buying guide that answers those questions realistically, by featuring the best wines in the broad marketplace, along with plenty of food-pairing advice to help you make the most of every wine purchase.

HOW THE GUIDE IS ORGANIZED
There are two ways to look up wines:

1. By Grape, Region, or Type

The Top Ten Wines tasting notes are grouped by major grape variety, region, or type, from sparkling to white to red, as follows:

2. Top Ten "At a Glance"

For quick-reference, the Top Ten wines in each category are shown at the front of the book starting on page 14.

In each section, the wines are listed alphabetically by winery name.

Key to the Ratings & Tasting Notes

The sample entry below identifies the components of each wine listing.

1. **The Facts** - Name, vintage & where it is from
2. **The Price** - the national average retail price from an excellent website that tracks and averages retailer prices (www.wine-searcher.com); Prices can vary a lot by market based on taxes and discount policies, but this will give you an idea of what to expect
3. **The Score** - on a 100-point scale; as with your grades in school, a 100 is perfect. (As I've pointed out, perfection in wine is subjective!)
4. **The Reviews** - My review, tasting notes and pairings for each wine.
5. **My Kitchen Survivor™** Grade
6. **Your notes** - Space for your wine notes.

---

❶ Chateau Andrea Rose 2008   ❷ $ ❸ Pts
New York   22   88

❹ Wine lovers marvel at this wine's amazing quality for a bag-in-the-box. I find it every bit as good as the finest Cold Duck ... and sometimes better!

❺ *Kitchen Survivor™ Grade:* A

❻ Your notes: _____

Kitchen Survivor™ Grades

Since "How long will it keep after I open it?" is one of the most common wine questions I'm asked, I decided it was time to give some solid answers.

And thus were born the Kitchen Survivor™ experiments. To test wines' open-bottle longevity, I handle them as follows:

Whites—Recorked with the original cork (whether natural or synthetic). Placed in the fridge.

Reds—Recorked with the original cork. Placed on the kitchen counter.

Sparkling wines—Opened carefully without popping (popping depletes carbonation faster).

Closed with a "clamshell" stopper designed for sparkling wines—sold in housewares departments and sometimes wine stores. Placed in the fridge.

The same process is repeated after each daily retaste, until the wine's taste declines noticeably.

I do this for every wine I taste that's a candidate for inclusion in the guide. The great news is that far more often than you'd think, the good wines stay that way for days. Even more interesting, some wines that seem initially under whelming actually come around and start tasting better after being open for awhile (in the same way that some cheeses need to sit out at room temperature to show their best flavor or a pot of chili can taste better after a day or two in the fridge). Based on these taste tests, I grade each wine as follows:

C = a "one-day wine," which tastes noticeably less fresh the next day. This doesn't mean the wine is less worthy, just less sturdy—so plan to finish it with tonight's dinner.

B = holds its freshness for 2–3 days after opening

B+ = holds *and gets better* over 2–3 days after opening

A = has a 3- to 4-day "freshness window"

A+ = holds *and gets better* over 3–4 days

I hope these grades will give you the confidence to enjoy wine more often with your everyday meals, knowing that in most cases the bottle won't go "bad" if you don't finish it right away.

Your Notes

The best way to learn about wine is to keep tasting, and keep notes. Whether you're at home or in a restaurant, the *Guide* is a handy place to keep track of what you drank, what you paid, what food you had with it, and what you thought. Don't you hate it when you've enjoyed a wine, then can't remember the name when you want to buy it again?

ANDREA'S TOP TEN WINES FOR EVERYONE

At a Glance

Name	Price	Score
Top 10 Sparkling WInes ($20 or less)		
Chandon Brut Classic	$16	91
Chandon Brut Rose NV	$18	90
Domaine Ste. Michelle Extra Dry NV	$12	88
Freixenet Brut de Noirs Rose NV	$10	89
Gloria Ferrer Sonoma Brut NV	$18	89
Mionetto Prosecco DOCG Brut NV	$16	88
Piper-Sonoma Brut, Sonoma NV	$16	93
Segura Viudas Aria Cava Brut NV	$16	88
Veuve du Vernay Brut NV	$14	90
Zardetto "Z" Prosecco Brut NV	$17	89
Top 10 Sparkling Wines (over $20)		
Adami Vigneto Giardino Prosecco 2009	$23	88
Bisol Crede Prosecco NV	$21	89
Ca' del Bosco Franciacortia Brut NV	$38	92
Domaine Carneros Brut 2006	$25	90
Domaine Carneros Le Reve Blanc de Blancs 2004	$25	93
Iron Horse Classic Vintage Brut 2005	$33	91
J Cuvee 20 Brut Sonoma NV	$35	91
Mionetto Cartizze Prosecco NV	$40	92
Roederer Estate Brut NV	$22	90
Schramsberg Blanc de Blancs 2007	$36	93
Top 10 French Champagnes ($50 and under)		
A. Margaine Cuvee Traditionelle Brut 1er Cru NV	$46	90
Chartogne-Taillet Cuvee Ste. Anne Brut NV	$44	93
Gaston Chiquet Brut Tradition NV	$48	90
Jacquart Brut Mosaique NV	$40	90
Louis Roederer Brut Premier NV	$40	91
Moët & Chandon Brut Imperial NV	$38	90
Piper-Heidsieck Brut Rose Sauvage NV	$50	97
Pierre Gimonnet 1er Cru Brut NV	$50	91

Pol Roger Extra Cuvee de		
Reserve 'Pure' NV	$40	91
Taittinger Brut La Française NV	$45	92

Top 10 French Champagnes (over $50)

Bollinger Brut Special Cuvee NV	$60	90
Charles Heidsieck Brut Reserve NV	$55	98
Dom Perignon Champagne Brut 2002	$165	96
G.H. Mumm de Cramant		
Blanc de Blancs NV	$55	93
Krug Grande Cuvee Multivintage	$165	96
Perrier-Jouët Fleur de Champagne		
Brut 2002	$139	94
Piper-Heidsieck Cuvee Brut 2002 NV	$65	93
Ruinart Blanc de Blancs Brut NV	$70	91
Taittinger Comtes de Champagne		
Blanc de Blancs 1999	$190	96
Veuve Clicquot Brut Rose 2004	$75	97

Top 10 Pinot Gris/Pinot Grigios

Alois Lageder Pinot Grigio,		
Alto Adige 2009	$18	89
Attems Pinot Grigio, Collio 2009	$16	93
Bollini Pinot Grigio Trentino 2009	$13	92
Clos du Bois Pinot Grigio 2008	$12	87
Cupcake Pinot Grigio 2009	$8	87
Hugel Pinot Gris "Classic,"		
Alsace 2009	$16	90
King Estate Signature Collection		
Pinot Gris 2009	$17	90
Livio Felluga Map Label		
Pinot Grigio 2009	$18	89
Pighin Pinot Grigio Grave 2009	$16	91
Woodbridge Pinot Grigio 2009	$8	87

Top 10 German Rieslings

Loosen Brothers "Dr. L" Riesling 2009	$12	88
Dr. Loosen Blue Slate Riesling 2009	23	90
Leitz Dragonstone 2009	$18	91
Leitz Eins Zwei Dry Riesling 2009	$16	92
Markus Molitor Haus Klosterberg		
Riesling Dry 2009	$16	91
Meulenhof Erdener Treppchen Riesling		
Spatlese Old Vines 2009	$19	94

Name	Price	Score

Top 10 German Rieslings (cont.)

Name	Price	Score
Prinz von Hessen Riesling 2008	$15	90
Robert Weil Estate Riesling Trocken 2009	$28	93
Saint M Riesling 2009	$12	90
Selbach-Oster Zeltinger Schlossberg Riesling Spatlese 2009	$30	94

Top 10 Rieslings: Alsace & Austria

Name	Price	Score
Brundlmayer Riesling Heiligenstein Alte Reben, Kamptal,2008	$50	94
Emmerich Knoll Riesling Smaragd 2008	$36	92
Hirsch Zobinger Heiligenstein Riesling 2008	$36	92
Domaine Weinbach Riesling Grand Cru, Schlossberg, Alsace 2008	$48	97
Hugel Riesling Jubilee, Alsace 2005	$30	94
Pierre Sparr Selection Riesling, Alsace 2008	$9	90
Prager Wachstum Bodenstein Riesling Smaragd 2008	$38	94
Trimbach Riesling, Alsace 2008	$18	91
Trimbach Riesling Cuvee Frederic Emile, Alsace 2005	$36	94
Zind-Humbrecht Riesling "Zind", Alsace 2008	$20	91

Top 10 New World Rieslings

Name	Price	Score
Barnard-Griffin 2009	$11	90
Chateau Ste. Michelle Dry Riesling 2009	$14	89
Eroica 2009	$22	94
Kendall-Jackson Vintner's Reserve 2009	$12	89
Jacob's Creek Reserve 2009	$14	90
Pacific Rim Dry Riesling 2009	$14	90
Robert Mondavi Private Selection 2009	$11	88
Smith-Madrone Riesling 2009	$27	90
Snoqualmie 'Naked' Riesling 2009	$10	88
Trefethen Estate Dry Riesling, 2009	$22	92

Name	Price	Score

Top 10 New World Sauvignon Blancs (under $15)

Name	Price	Score
Brancott, Marlborough 2009	$11	89
Casa Lapostolle, Chile 2009	$10	89
Chateau Ste. Michelle Horse Heaven Hills 2009	$14	90
Dry Creek Vineyard Fume Blanc 2009	$12	89
Joel Gott 2009	$10	89
Kendall-Jackson Vintner's Reserve 2008	$12	89
Nobilo Regional Collection 2009	$10	89
Veramonte, Chile 2009	$12	90
Wente Louis Mel 2009	$11	90
Woodbridge 2009	$6	88

Top 10 New World Sauvignon Blancs (15-$25)

Name	Price	Score
Cliff Lede 2009	$20	93
Benziger 2009	$16	89
Frog's Leap 2009	$18	90
Girard 2009	$16	NA*
Matanzas Creek 2009	$24	92
Morgan 2009	$16	90
Mulderbosch 2009	$17	92
Robert Mondavi Fume Blanc 2008	$20	94
St. Supery 2009	$23	93
Silverado Miller Ranch 2009	$22	94

Top 10 New World Sauvignon Blancs ($25 and up)

Name	Price	Score
Araujo 2009	$40	95
Chalk Hill 2008	$28	95
Delille Chaleur Estate Blanc 2009	$34	94
Duckhorn 2009	$25	90
Flora Springs Soliloquy 2009	$25	92
Grgich Hills Fume Blanc 2009	$28	94
Robert Mondavi Fume Blanc Reserve To-Ka-Lon Vineyard 2008	$40	94
Merry Edwards 2009	$30	95
Spottswoode 2009	$35	90
Rochioli 2009	$39	94

*We sell our vineyard's grapes to this winery so I have not given it a score but, I highly recommend it!

Name	Price	Score

Top 10 Old World & New Zealand Sauvignon Blancs

Name	Price	Score
Brancott Reserve 2009	$18	91
Cloudy Bay 2009	$26	90
Cloudy Bay Te Koko 2006	$55	92
Chateau Carbonnieux 2007	$34	89
Chateau de Sancerre 2008	$19	89
Chateau Loudenne Blanc 2007	$20	90
Jolivet Sancerre 2009	$22	89
Kim Crawford 2009	$19	89
Pastou Sancerre	$17	92
Villa Maria Cellar Selection	$18	89

Top 10 New World Chardonnays ($12 & under)

Name	Price	Score
Cellar No. 8 2008	$11	90
Clos du Bois, North Coast 2009	$12	89
Hess Select, Monterey 2009	$10	89
Jacob's Creek Reserve 2009	$12	90
Lockwood, Monterey 2008	$11	88
Main Street, Santa Barbara County 2008	$11	89
McWilliam's Hanwood Estate 2009	$10	90
Penfolds Koonunga Hill 2009	$12	89
Wolf Blass Yellow Label 2009	$9	89
Woodbridge 2009	$8	87

Top 10 New World Chardonnays ($12 to $20)

Name	Price	Score
Au Bon Climat Santa Barbara 2009	$20	92
Calera Central Coast 2009	$17	93
Cambria Katherine's Vineyard 2008	$20	89
Chateau Ste. Michelle Indian Wells 2008	$18	91
Clos du Bois Sonoma Reserve 2007	$17	91
Chateau St. Jean 2009	$13	89
Kali Hart, Monterey 2009	$19	94
Kendall-Jackson Vintner's Reserve 2009	$14	89:
Souverain, Alexander Valley 2009	$17	90
Wente Riva Ranch 2009	$17	90

Name	Price	Score

Top 10 New World Chardonnays ($20 to $40-Napa)

Name	Price	Score
Beringer Private Reserve 2008	$35	90
Chappellet 2008	$32	92
Flora Springs Barrel Fermented 2008	$23	90
Franciscan Cuvee Sauvage 2007	$36	92
Frank Family 2008	$33	93
Robert Mondavi Napa 2008	$20	89
Rombauer, Carneros 2008	$34	88
St. Supery Oak Free 2008	$19	89
Stag's Leap Wine Cellars Karia 2008	$34	90
Trefethen Estate 2008	$30	93

Top 10 New World Chardonnays ($20 to $40-Other)

Name	Price	Score
Catena Alta 2008	$25	90
Chalk Hill Estate 2008	$35	97
Chateau Ste. Michelle Cold Creek 2008	$22	90
Chateau St. Jean Robert Young 2007	$25	92
Matanzas Creek 2008	$29	92
Mer Soleil 'Silver' Unoaked 2008	$26	94
Rodney Strong Reserve 2007	$40	91
Sonoma-Cutrer Russian River Ranches 2009	$21	91
Sbragia Family Home Ranch 2008	$26	92
Talbott (Robert) Sleepy Hollow 2008	$38	95

Top 10 New World Chardonnays ($40 and up)

Name	Price	Score
Antinori Cervaro della Sala 2008	$50	95
Far Niente Estate Bottled 2008	$56	90
Grgich Hills Estate 2008	$42	94
Kistler Vine Hill Vineyard 2007	$125	94
Leeuwin Estate Art Series 2006	$89	94
Newton Unfiltered 2007	$48	92
Ramey Wine Cellars Hyde Vineyard 2007	$60	96
Ridge Vineyard Santa Cruz Mountains Estate 2008	$40	97
Shafer Red Shoulder Ranch 2008	$48	95
Staglin Family Estate 2008	$75	96

Top 10 Chardonnays: French White Burgundy

Name	Price	Score
Cave de Lugny Macon-Lugny 'Les Charmes' 2008	$11	89
Chartron & Trebuchet Rully La Chaume 2008	$18	89
Joseph Drouhin Pouilly-Fuisse 2008	$30	89
Domaine Laroche Chablis St. Martin 2008	$30	89
Domaine Leflaive Puligny-Montrachet 2008	$100	92
Domaine Vincent Girardin Pouilly-Fuisse Vieilles Vignes 2009	$28	90
M. Colin Saint-Aubin En Remilly 2008	$35	93
Louis Jadot Pouilly-Fuisse 2008	$24	89
Louis Latour Corton-Charlemagne 2008	$95	95
Olivier Leflaive Meursault 2008	$40	91

Top 10 Uncommon Whites: Alsace & Austria

Name	Price	Score
Albert Boxler Muscat Grand Cru Brand, Alsace 2008	$40	97
Brundlmayer Gruner-Veltliner Kamptaler Terrassen 2009	$19	94
Heidi Schrock Ried Vogelsang blend 2009	$16	90
Fred Loimer 'Lois' Gruner-Veltliner 2009	$12	89
Hugel Pinot Blanc Cuvee Les Amours, Alsace 2009	$15	91
Laurenz "Singing" Gruner-Veltliner 2009	$15	90
Nigl Gruner-Veltliner Alte Reben, Kremstal 2009	$30	94
Pierre Sparr Pinot Blanc Reserve 2008	$14	90
Schloss Gobelsburg Gruner-Veltliner Gobelsburger 2009	$14	92
Setzer Gruner Veltliner Ausstich 2009	$16	9

Name	Price	Score

Top 10 Uncommon Whites: New World

Name	Price	Score
Crios Torrontes 2009	$14	90
Dry Creek Vineyard Dry Chenin Blanc 2009	$11	88
Fetzer Valley Oaks Gewurztraminer 2008	$7	87
Gougenheim Torrontes 2009	$12	90
Kanu Chenin Blanc 2009	$9	89
Miner Family Viognier Simpson Vineyard 2008	$20	94
Qupe Marsanne 2009	$18	94
Sokol Blosser Evolution NV	$15	89
Tablas Creek Cotes de Tablas Blanc 2008	$22	91
Zaca Mesa Viognier 2008	$19	91

Top 10 Uncommon Whites: Old World

Name	Price	Score
Bastianich Friulano, Friuli 2008	$18	90
Guado al Tasso Vermentino 2009	$22	91
Inama "Vin Soave" Classico 2008	$17	90
Hidalgo La Gitana Manzanilla Sherry NV	$16	90
Lopez de Heredia Rioja Blanco 2000	$25	92
Marques de Riscal Rueda 2009	$9	89
Martin Codax Albarino, Rias Baixas 2009	$15	89
Palacios Remondo Placet Rioja Blanco 2007	$23	89
Sella & Mosca La Cala Vermentino 2009	$13	89
Villa Sparina Gavi di Gavi 2009	$17	90

Top 10 Rosés

Name	Price	Score
Bodegas Muga Rioja Rosado 2009	$12	89
Bodegas Ochoa Rosado 2009	$9	88
Bonny Doon Vin Gris de Cigare Pink Wine 2009	$12	89
Chateau d'Aqueria Tavel Rose 2009	$19	90
Chateau d'Eclans Whispering Angel Rosé 2009	$18	89
Domaine Tempier Bandol Rosé 2009	$35	92
El Coto Rioja Rosado 2009	$11	91

Name	Price	Score

Top 10 Rosés (cont.)

Etude Pinot Noir Rosé 2009	$16	91
Lopez de Heredia Tondonia Rioja		
Rosado Gran Reserva 2000	$26	93
Miner Family Sangiovese Rosato		
Gibson Ranch 2009	$16	92

Top 10 California Pinot Noir (under $20)

Au Bon Climat		
Santa Maria Valley 2008	$18	93
Brancott Vineyards South Island 2009	$14	89
Carmel Road 2008	$17	89
Castle Rock, Mendocino 2009	$14	90
Chateau St. Jean Sonoma 2008	$19	90
Kendall-Jackson		
Vintner's Reserve 2009	$18	89
Lindemans Bin 99 2009	$9	88
Mark West 2009	$15	89
Robert Mondavi Private		
Selection 2008	$11	88
Rosemount Diamond Label 2009	$11	87

Top 10 California Pinot Noirs ($20-$40)

Calera Central Coast 2008	$24	93
Cambria Julia's Vineyard 2008	$22	90
Deloach Russian River 2008	$24	89
Dutton-Goldfield Dutton Ranch 2008	$38	92
Etude Carneros 2008	$40	96
La Crema Russian River Valley 2008	$22	92
Lynmar Russian River	$40	93
MacMurray Ranch		
Central Coast 2008	$20	90
Meiomi by Belle Glos		
Sonoma Coast 2008	$25	93
Robert Mondavi Los Carneros 2008	$27	93

Top 10 California Pinot Noirs (over $40)

Au Bon Climat Isabel 2007	$47	96
Benovia 2008	$42	91
Calera Selleck 2006	$65	96
Goldeneye 2007	$55	92
Merry Edwards Olivet Lane 2008	$60	100

Name	Price	Score
Miner Garys' Vineyard 2008	$52	91
Peay Estate Pinot Noir 2008	$48	94
Pfendler Sonoma Coast 2007	$44	96
Rochioli Russian River 2008	$62	93
Williams-Selyem Russian River 2008	$45	96

Top 10 Oregon & Other New World Pinot Noirs

Name	Price	Score
Brancott Reserve 2007	$20	90
Clos Henri 2007	$35	92
Coldstream Hills 2007	$29	89
Cristom Mt. Jefferson Cuvee 2008	$29	93
Domaine Drouhin Oregon 2008	$40	90
Domaine Serene Evenstad Reserve 2007	$65	91
Penfolds Cellar Reserve 2007	$44	92
Ponzi 2008	$35	89
Sokol-Blosser Dundee Hills 2007	$38	92
Willamette Valley Vineyards Founder's Reserve 2007	$28	89

Top 10 Pinot Noirs: French Burgundy

Name	Price	Score
Domaine Albert Bichot Mercurey 2009	$24	90
Domaine Joblot Givry Cellier aux Moines 2007	$42	90
Domaine Daniel Rion Nuits St. Georges Grandes Vignes 2007	$49	90
Joseph Drouhin Cote de Beaune 2007	$36	91
Joseph Faiveley Gevrey-Chambertin 2008	$55	91
Joseph Faiveley Mercurey Clos des Myglands 2008	$29	89
Louis Latour Marsannay 2007	$17	88
Louis Jadot Beaune Clos des Ursules 2007	$55	93
Marquis d'Angerville Volnay 2007	$50	94
Nicolas Potel Savigny-les-Beaune 2007	$40	91

Top 10 Italian Reds ($25 or less)

Name	Price	Score
Avignonesi Rosso di Montepulciano 2009	$18	90

Name	Price	Score

Top 10 Italian Reds $25 or less (cont.)

Name	Price	Score
Badia a Coltibuono Chianti Classico 2007	$25	89
Castello di Gabbiano Chianti Classico 2007	$13	88
Dievole Chianti Classico Vendemmia 2007	$19	90
Falesco Vitiano 2009	$12	89
Frescobaldi Nipozzano Chianti Rufina Riserva 2007	$25	91
Marchesi di Gresy Monte Aribaldo Dolcetto d'Alba 2007	$17	89
Michele Chiarlo Barbera d'Asti 'Le Orme' 2007	$15	90
Taurino Salice Salentino Rosso Riserva 2007	$12	89
Vietti Barbera d'Asti Tre Vigne 2008	$17	89

Top 10 Italian Reds (above $25)

Name	Price	Score
Badia a Coltibuono Sangioveto 2003	$60	90
Castelgiocondo Brunello di Montalcino (Frescobaldi) 2005	$52	90
Castellare di Castellina Chianti Classico Riserva 2007	$28	90
Castello di Ama Chianti Classico 2007	$36	92
Ceretto Zonchera Barolo 2005	$51	91
Marchese Antinori Chianti Classico Riserva 2007	$35	89
Marchesi di Gresy Barbaresco Martinenga 2006	$60	92
Ruffino Chianti Classico Riserva Ducale Oro 2006	$40	91
Val di Suga Brunello di Montalcino 2004	$66	94
Val di Suga Rosso di Montalcino 2006	$26	91

Top 10 Super Tuscans

Name	Price	Score
Castello Banfi Cum Laude 2006	$35	89
Castello di Gabbiano Alleanza 2007	$35	93
Guado al Tasso 2006	$115	95
La Vite Lucente 2007	$25	91

Name	Price	Score
Luce della Vite 2006	$80	94
Ornellaia 2006	$125	93
Solaia (Antinori) 2007	$270	97
Tenuta del Terriccio Tassinaia 2006	$35	90
Tenuta Sette Ponti Crognolo 2008	$35	92
Tignanello 2007	$95	95

Top 10 Merlots ($25 or less)

Name	Price	Score
Chateau St. Jean, Sonoma 2007	$25	91
Chateau Ste. Michelle Indian Wells 2008	$18	91
Clos du Bois North Coast 2007	$17	89
Columbia Crest Grand Estates 2008	$10	87
Fetzer Valley Oaks 2008	$9	86
Ravenswood Vintners Blend 2008	$10	89
Raymond Reserve 2006	$24	90
Sebastiani Sonoma County 2007	$17	90
Souverain Alexander Valley 2007	$19	90
Sterling Vineyards 2007	$22	89

Top 10 Merlots (above $25)

Name	Price	Score
Beringer Bancroft Ranch, Howell Mountain 2006	$75	97
Duckhorn, Napa 2007	$46	92
Frog's Leap, Rutherford 2007	$34	91
Grgich Hills Estate, Napa 2006	$42	92
L'Ecole No. 41 Seven Hills Vineyard Estate 2007	$36	91
Newton Unfiltered, Napa 2006	$50	91
Northstar Walla Walla 2006	$40	93
St. Clement, Napa 2007	$28	94
Shafer, Napa 2007	$46	91
Silverado, Napa 2007	$35	90

Top 10 New World Cabernets (under $20)

Name	Price	Score
Clos du Bois, Sonoma 2007	$14	88
Baron Philippe de Rothschild, Escudo Rojo Cabernet Blend, Chile 2007	$14	91
Jacob's Creek Reserve, Australia 2008	$12	91
Los Vascos, Chile 2008	$10	90
Louis Martini, Sonoma 2007	$16	89

Name	Price	Score

Top 10 New World Cabernets under $20 (cont.)

Name	Price	Score
Ravenswood Vintners Blend 2008	$10	89
Rosemount Diamond Label 2009	$10	88
Santa Rita 120, Chile 2009	$8	89
Sebastiani, Sonoma 2007	$16	91
Veramonte Reserva, Chile 2008	$13	90

Top 10 New World Cabernets ($20 to $45)

Name	Price	Score
Antu Ninquen Cabernet Sauvignon-Carmenere, Chile 2008	$22	93
Beringer Knights Valley 2007	$22	93
Catena Zapata, Argentina 2007	$45	94
Cousino-Macul Antiguas Reservas, Chile 2008	$22	90
Chateau Ste. Michelle Indian Wells 2008	$28	90
Chateau St. Jean, Sonoma 2006	$27	92
Clos du Bois Reserve, Alexander Valley 2007	$22	91
Louis Martini Alexander Valley Reserve 2007	$32	91
Penfolds Bin 389 Cabernet Shiraz, South Australia 2007	$37	97
Souverain Alexander Valley 2006	$20	90

Top 10 New World Cabernets (above $45)

Name	Price	Score
Chalk Hill Estate, Sonoma 2007	$70	97
Chateau St. Jean Cinq Cepages Cabernet Blend, Sonoma 2006	$75	90
Col Solare Red Blend, Columbia Valley 2007	$55	91
Concha y Toro Don Melchor Reserva, Chile 2007	$70	91
Jordan, Alexander Valley 2006	$50	89
Justin Isosceles 2007	$62	93
Leonetti Cellar, Washington 2007	$85	94
Penfolds Bin 707 2007	$140	98
Rodney Strong Symmetry Meritage, Alexander Valley 2007	$60	92
Silver Oak Alexander Valley 2006	$70	91

Name	Price	Score

Top 10 Napa Cabernets (under $45)

Name	Price	Score
Beaulieu Rutherford 2007	$26	90
Beringer Alluvium 2007	$30	91
Chappellet Signature 2007	$42	94
Faust 2007	$44	92
Flora Springs Napa 2007	$32	91
Franciscan Magnificat Meritage 2006	$43	89
Frog's Leap 2007	$42	91
Louis Martini Napa Reserve 2007	$25	90
Robert Mondavi 2007	$28	91
St. Clement 2007	$35	94

Top 10 Napa Cabernets ($45 & up)

Name	Price	Score
Caymus 2008	$70	90
BV Tapestry Reserve 2007	$55	91
Frank Family Vineyards 2007	$45	96
Grgich Hills Estate 2006	$60	92
Heitz Cellars, Napa 2006	$45	94
Ladera, Howell Mountain 2007	$60	97
Mt. Veeder 2007	$50	91
Beaulieu (BV) Georges de Latour Private Reserve 2007	$80	95
Silver Oak Napa Valley 2005	$100	94
Trefethen Estate 2007	$50	94

Top 10 California Cabernets (over $100)

Name	Price	Score
Araujo, Eisele Vineyard 2007	$250	99
Beringer Private Reserve 2007	$116	93
Dalla Valle, Oakville 2006	$150	94
Etude, Napa 2006	$125	98
Heitz Cellars Martha's Vineyard 2005	$150	97
Ridge Monte Bello 2007	$145	100
Robert Mondavi Reserve 2007	$135	96
Shafer Hillside Select 2006	$215	96
Staglin Family Estate 2007	$175	100
Stag's Leap Cask 23 2007	$195	99

Top 10 French Red Bordeaux under $50

Name	Price	Score
Chateau d'Angludet, Margaux 2007	$28	93
Chateau Beaumont, Haut-Medoc 2007	$25	91

Top 10 French Red Bordeaux under $50 (cont.)

	Price	Score
Chateau Chasse-Spleen, Moulis-en-Medoc 2007	$35	91
Chateau Cantemerle, Haut-Medoc 2007	$31	89
Chateau de Pez, Saint-Estephe 2007	$42	95
Chateau Greysac, Medoc 2007	$22	88
Chateau Marquis de Terme, Margaux 2007	$45	91
Chateau Ormes de Pez, Saint-Estephe 2007	$31	94
Chateau Poujeaux, Moulis-en-Medoc 2007	$29	90
Chateau du Tertre, Margaux 2007	$35	92

Top 10 French Red Bordeaux ($50 & up)

	Price	Score
Chateau Angelus, Saint-Emilion 2007	$180	96
Chateau Beychevelle, Saint-Julien 2007	$54	91
Chateau Canon, Saint-Emilion 2007	$65	93
Chateau Clinet, Pomerol 2007	$60	92
Chateau Gazin, Pomerol 2007	$54	91
Giscours, Margaux 2007	$60	90
Chateau Lascombes, Margaux 2007	$60	93
Chateau Leoville-Poyferre, Saint-Julien 2007	$63	91
Chateau Lynch-Bages, Pauillac 2007	$77	96
Clos Fourtet, Saint-Emilion 2007	$50	93

Top 10 Spanish Reds ($25 or less)

	Price	Score
Abadia Retuerta Rivola 2008	$14	89
Abadia Retuerta Seleccion Especial 2007	$20	91
Bodegas O. Fournier Urban Ribera del Duero Roble 2007	$14	90
Bordon Rioja Gran Reserva 2001	$24	92
Borsao Tinto Garnacha/ Tempranillo 2009	$8	88
El Coto de Imaz Rioja Reserva 2004	$15	91
Faustino V Rioja Reserva 2004	$20	94

Name	Price	Score
Federico Tinto Ribera del Duero 2007	$17	90
Mibal Ribera del Duero 2006	$14	89
Palacios Remondo La Montesa Rioja Crianza 2007	$20	89

Top 10 Spanish Reds (above $25)

Name	Price	Score
Aalto Ribera del Duero 2007	$54	92
Baron de Ley Rioja Gran Reserva 1998	$38	96
Bohorquez Ribera del Duero 2005	$34	91
La Rioja Alta Vina Ardanza Reserva 2000	$35	92
Marqués de Murrieta Castillo Ygay Rioja Gran Reserva Especial 2001	$54	96
Marqués de Riscal Rioja Gran Reserva 2000	$35	90
Muga Rioja Reserva 2006	$26	92
Pesquera Crianza, Ribera del Duero 2006	$35	91
R. Lopez de Heredia Vina Bosconia Rioja Reserva 2001	$36	94
Teofilo Reyes Ribera del Duero 2004	$63	94

Top 10 Uncommon Red Grapes

Name	Price	Score
Argento Malbec 2008	$9	89
Casa Lapostolle Carmenere 2008	$9	92
Duboeuf (Georges) Beaujolais Villages 2009	$12	90
Bogle Petite Sirah 2008	$12	89
Catena Alta Malbec 2007	$40	92
Concannon 'The Conservancy' Petite Sirah 2007	$12	89
Lang & Reed Cabernet Franc '214' 2007	$40	92
Miner Family Sangiovese Gibson Ranch 2007	$20	91
Salentein Malbec Reserve 2007	$20	90
Veramonte Primus 2007	$17	90

Name	Price	Score

Top 10 New World Syrah/Shiraz ($20 and under)

Name	Price	Score
Alice White Shiraz 2008	$6	87
D'Arenberg The Footbolt Shiraz 2008	$15	89
Jacob's Creek Reserve Shiraz 2007	$11	90
Jacob's Creek Shiraz/Cabernet 2007	$8	89
Morgan Monterey Syrah 2008	$18	90
Penfolds Koonunga Hill Shiraz/ Cabernet 2008	$11	88
Qupe Central Coast Syrah 2008	$17	93
Rosemount Diamond Label Shiraz/Cabernet 2008	$10	89
Wente Syrah Livermore 2008	$12	89
Wolf-Blass Yellow Label Shiraz 2008	$9	89

Top 10 New World Syrah/Shiraz (above $20)

Name	Price	Score
Cape Mentelle Shiraz 2006	$30	93
Fleming-Jenkins Santa Cruz Syrah 2007	$37	91
Kendall-Jackson Highland Estates Alisos Hills Syrah 2006	$35	94
Lynmar Russian River Syrah 2007	$36	92
Morgan Double L Syrah 2007	$40	93
Penfolds Kalimna Bin 28 Shiraz 2007	$25	91
Penfolds St. Henri Shiraz 2006	$60	95
Rosemount Show Reserve GSM 2006	$24	90
Tablas Creek Cotes de Tablas Red Blend 2008	$25	91
Zaca Mesa Santa Ynez Syrah 2006	$23	90

Top 10 French Syrah/Rhone Reds

Name	Price	Score
Alain Graillot Crozes-Hermitage 2007	$34	92
Chapoutier Cotes-du-Rhone Belleruche 2008	$11	89
Chapoutier Hermitage Monier de la Sizeranne 2007	$90	91
Coudoulet de Beaucastel Cotes-du-Rhone 2008	$25	90
Domaine du Vieux Telegraphe Chateauneuf-du-Pape 2007	$70	94

Name	Price	Score
Domaine Grand Veneur Chateauneuf-du-Pape 2007	$45	92
E & M Guigal Cote-Rotie Brune et Blonde 2006	$57	94
E & M Guigal Cotes-du-Rhone 2007	$12	89
Jaboulet Parallele 45 Cotes-du-Rhone 2008	$14	89
La Vieille Ferme Cotes-du-Ventoux 2008	$9	88

Top 10 Red Zinfandels

Name	Price	Score
7 Deadly Zins Lodi 2008	$9	87
Bogle Old Vines 2008	$11	87
Frank Family 2008	$35	94
Frog's Leap 2008	$28	91
Grgich Hills 2007	$30	93
Joel Gott 2008	$14	88
Martinelli Vellutini Ranch 2007	$60	91
Ravenswood Lodi Old Vines 2007	$14	90
Ridge Lytton Springs 2008	$40	94
Storybook Mountain Mayacamas 2008	$30	91

Top 10 Dessert Wines

Name	Price	Score
Blandy's 10 Year Malmsey Madeira NV	$33	92
Calem 10 year Tawny Porto NV	$30	91
Castello Banfi Brachetto d'Acqui Rosa Regale, Italy 2009	$20	91
Chambers Rosewood Rutherglen Muscadelle NV	$15	91
Chateau Coutet, Barsac-Sauternes 2007	$55	93
Chateau du Cros Loupiac 2007	$14	90
Chateau La Tour Blanche Sauternes 2007	$60	94
Chateau Ste. Michelle Ethos Late Harvest Riesling 2006	$32	92
Ferreira Dona Antonia Tawny Porto NV	$18	90
Pacific Rim Selenium Vineyard Riesling Vin de Glaciere 2007	$15	90

THE REVIEWS

CHAMPAGNE & SPARKLING WINE

Style Profile: Although all the world's bubblies are modeled on Champagne, only the genuine article from the Champagne *region* of France is properly called *Champagne. Sparkling wine* is the proper term for the other bubblies, some of which can be just as good as the real thing. Limited supply and high demand—plus a labor-intensive production process—make Champagne expensive compared to other sparklers but still an affordable luxury in comparison to other world-class wine categories, like top French Burgundy or California Cabernet estates. The other sparklers, especially Cava from Spain and Italian Prosecco, are affordable for everyday drinking. *Brut* (rhymes with *root*) on the label means the wine is utterly dry, with no perceptible sweetness. But that *doesn't* mean they all taste the same. In fact, each French Champagne house is known for a signature style, which can range from delicate and elegant to rich, full, and toasty—meaning there's something for every taste and food partner.

Serve: Well chilled; young and fresh (only the rare luxury French Champagnes improve with age). Open with utmost care: flying corks can be dangerous.

When: Anytime! Bubbly is not just for special occasions, and it's great with meals. Rose even matches meat and poultry.

With: Anything and anyone, but especially sushi, shellfish, fried foods and popcorn.

In: Classically, a narrow tulip- or flute-type glass is used because the narrow opening preserves the bubbles. Having said that, after testing out my The One white wine stem, several Master Sommeliers, to my surprise, recommended it for Champagne and bubbly. I tried it and was quite amazed at how much more fragrance and depth of flavor get showcased by the white wine stem.

Kitchen Survivor™ Tip for Bubbly Wine: Kitchenware shops and wine stores often sell "clamshell" stoppers specially designed to close Champagnes and sparkling wines if you don't finish the bottle. I've found that if you open the bottle carefully in the first place (avoid "popping" the cork, which is also the safest technique), a stoppered sparkling wine will keep its fizz for at least three days in the fridge, often much longer. Having a hard time thinking of something else to toast? How about, "Here's to [insert day of week]." That's usually good enough for me!

Will the real Champagne please stand up?

As the saying goes, all Champagne is sparkling wine, but not all sparkling wine is Champagne...

Much of the cheapest American-made sparkling wine is labeled "champagne," as a generic term for a wine with bubbles (these don't make my "Top Ten"). But of course true Champagne, coming from the Champagne region of France, is anything but generic in character, pedigree and quality. Our French friends will thank us if you don't buy those wines or at least, try not to refer to everything with bubbles as "champagne." Let's all try to remember to call it sparkling wine, ok? Merci!

TOP TEN SPARKLING WINES: $20 OR LESS

Chandon Brut Classic,   **Pts**
Napa, California NV   **$16**   **91**

Here's to a big-selling brand that doesn't cut quality corners. Chandon is packing loads of grilled pineapple and toasty biscuit flavors into every drop. Drinks like you paid double, so splurge & pair with crab!

Kitchen Survivor™ Grade: B+

Your notes: _____

Chandon Brut Rose,   **Pts**
Napa, California NV   **$18**   **90**

Consistently one of the best and best-value California roses on the market, with delicious spicy cherry and red currant fruit that's awesome with barbecue.

Kitchen Survivor™ Grade: B

Your notes: _____

Domaine Ste. Michelle Extra Dry   **Pts**
Sparkling, Washington NV   **$12**   **88**

This perennial value is tasting better than ever! It's rich and appley with just a little whisper of that Champagne-style toastiness that matches so well with fried foods and buttery flavors - think popcorn (steal) or lobster with drawn butter (splurge).

Kitchen Survivor™ Grade: B

Your notes: _____

Freixenet (*fresh-uh-NETT*) Brut   **Pts**
de Noirs, Cava Rose, Spain NV   **$10**   **89**

A juicy taste of tangy strawberries that's great with spicy tuna sushi, barbecue, and anything else with a kick. An amazing deal that's worth the search.

Kitchen Survivor™ Grade: A+

Your notes: _____

Gloria Ferrer Sonoma Brut,   **Pts**
California NV   **$18**   **89**

Crisp Anjou pear with a savory/earthy note and crisp acidity that pairs beautifully with both the briniest oysters and the sweetest clams and shrimp.

Kitchen Survivor™ Grade: A

Your notes: _____

Mionetto Prosecco Brut DOCG,   **Pts**
Veneto, Italy NV, $16   88

Dry and refreshing, with a juicy-apple mid-palate that makes it great on its own, and a savory minerality on the finish that pairs deliciously with pungent or salty antipasti (sausage, cheese, olives).

Kitchen Survivor™ Grade: A

Your notes: _____

Piper-Sonoma Brut Sparkling, Sonoma,   **Pts**
California NV $16   93

It's pretty super when one of the top CA sparklers is also one of the cheapest. This wine has amazing concentration, with deep apple, toasty biscuit and creme brulee flavors that are so yummy on their own you don't need food. But, it will go with ANYTHING!

Kitchen Survivor™ Grade: A+

Your notes: _____

Segura Viudas Aria Estate Cava Brut,   **Pts**
Penedes, Spain NV $16   88

A value star that looks and tastes super-classy. It's got gorgeous pear fruit and a round and creamy texture that begs for a silky partner - pate or scallops!

Kitchen Survivor™ Grade: A

Your notes: _____

Veuve du Vernay Brut,   **Pts**
France NV $14   90

Champagne-like brioche and apple tart flavors - in a value bubbly? That is why I chose it for Delta. The quality absolutely blew my mind. A stunning match for aged Gouda or Cheddar. *Merci* to the French!

Kitchen Survivor™ Grade: A

Your notes: _____

Zardetto "Z" Prosecco Brut,   **Pts**
Veneto, Italy NV $17   89

Keep a bottle of this crisp, totally dry and refreshing bubbly in the chiller at all times for impromptu company or an attitude adjustment after a bad day. Add bivalves and unleash your inner Venetian!

Kitchen Survivor™ Grade: A

Your notes: _____

TOP TEN SPARKLING WINES: OVER $20

Adami Vigneto Giardino Prosecco,   **Pts**
Veneto, Italy 2009   **$23**   **88**

A top Prosecco from an artisan producer. The rich pear fruit intensity on the palate makes it a perfect match for spicy sushi, Thai food or even teriyaki. *Kitchen Survivor™ Grade: B*

Your notes: _____

Bisol Crede Prosecco,   **Pts**
Veneto, Italy NV   **$21**   **89**

A sommelier favorite Prosecco thanks to its unexpected complexity. The fresh hay, dried flower, citrus peel and fresh apple notes keep you coming back to the glass. A great match for salads and charcuterie. *Kitchen Survivor™ Grade: B*

Your notes: _____

Ca' del Bosco Franciacorta Brut,   **Pts**
Lombardy, Italy NV   **$44**   **92**

Made in the Champagne style and totally dry, with subtle bread dough, cream, toast and fresh almond notes. The tingly-creamy mouthfeel makes it a great match for eggs Benedict or lemon cream-sauced fish. *Kitchen Survivor™ Grade: B+*

Your notes: _____

Domaine Carneros Brut,   **Pts**
Carneros, California 2006   **$25**   **90**

This is always one of the most elegant California bubblies, with biscuity, floral and candied lemon notes. Delicious with smoked salmon and yes, caviar. *Kitchen Survivor™ Grade: B*

Your notes: _____

Domaine Carneros Le Reve Blanc de Blancs   **Pts**
Brut, Carneros, California 2004   **$25**   **93**

Fragrant buttermilk biscuit and fresh butter scents, with a light toastiness and lovely finesse that make it bewitching on its own but also lovely with food – anything from seared scallops to aged Gouda cheese. *Kitchen Survivor™ Grade: A*

Your notes: _____

Iron Horse Classic Vintage Brut, Green   **Pts**
Valley (of RRV), California 2005   **$33**   **91**

Although Wedding Cuvee is the signature wine, this has become my true love from Iron Horse, for its toastiness, baked apple dumpling flavors, and length.

Kitchen Survivor™ Grade: B

Your notes: _____

J Cuvee 20 Brut, Sonoma,   **Pts**
California NV   **$35**   **91**

The signature flavor profile - quince paste and lemongrass - showcases the cool climate Russian River grapes, and the let-the-fruit show winemaking. It's a lovely match for spicy, barbecue & teriyaki flavors.

Kitchen Survivor™ Grade: A

Your notes: _____

Mionetto Cartizze Prosecco, Veneto,   **Pts**
Italy NV   **$40**   **92**

The hilly 'Cartizze' vineyard near Valdobbiadene yields top Proseccos like this one with creamy-tangy scents and flavors of baking scones and mascarpone, and a touch of chalkiness-perfect to pair with oysters.

Kitchen Survivor™ Grade: A

Your notes: _____

Roederer Estate Brut,   **Pts**
Anderson Valley, California NV   **$22**   **90**

To impress without breaking the bank, pour this. The full, toasty, baked apple flavors and classy, creamy palate show the family resemblance to its French parent Champagne Roederer. Great with mushroom pasta.

Kitchen Survivor™ Grade: A

Your notes: _____

Schramsberg Blanc de Blancs,   **Pts**
North Coast, California 2007   **$36**   **93**

This 100% Chardonnay bottling is all lacy-racy texture, with a mushroom bisque-y complexity and looong finish! Pair with fine cheeses or pate.

Kitchen Survivor™ Grade: A

Your notes: _____

TOP TEN FRENCH
CHAMPAGNE: $50 OR LESS

A. Margaine Cuvee Traditionelle Brut   Pts
1er Cru, Champagne, France NV $46   90

A grower Champagne that's worth the search. Elegant and lacy, with charged-up acidity and crisp citrus and pear notes plus a hint of mushroomy savoriness.
Kitchen Survivor™ Grade: A
Your notes: _____

Chartogne-Taillet Cuvee Ste. Anne Brut,   Pts
Champagne, France NV $44   93

An amazing value for the quality, and fun because it is made by a tiny artisan producer. It is toasty, nutty, smoky! A great match for smoked turkey or duck.
Kitchen Survivor™ Grade: A
Your notes: _____

Gaston Chiquet Brut Tradition,   Pts
Champagne, France NV $48   90

A favorite of sommeliers for its laser purity and expression of red fruit: currants, snappy red cherry. A "foodie's" bubbly that's seductive with duck confit, grilled quail or a simple roast chicken with herbs.
Kitchen Survivor™ Grade: A
Your notes: _____

Jacquart Brut Mosaique,   Pts
Champagne, France NV $40   90

The sommelier at Air France tipped me off to this bottle. I chose it for Delta because the rich scents of poundcake and brioche, and the spicy apple compote flavors will stand out even at altitude. Delicious on its own and with cheeses and warm nuts.
Kitchen Survivor™ Grade: A
Your notes: _____

Louis Roederer Brut Premier,   Pts
Champagne, France NV $40   91

One of the fullest-bodied non-vintage Champagnes, with scents of almond croissant, persimmon and quince, and a mouth-filling apple buttery, toasty-richness on the palate. Great with Thanksgiving turkey.
Kitchen Survivor™ Grade: A
Your notes: _____

Moët & Chandon Brut Imperial   **Pts**
Champagne, France NV   **$38   90**

This deserves its huge fan club for the quality and
consistency. It's medium-bodied and creamy, with
buttermilk biscuit and chamomile scents, and spiced
apple dumpling flavors. Pair with fried chicken!
Kitchen Survivor™ Grade: B
Your notes: _____

Piper-Heidsieck (*HIDE-sick*) Brut   **Pts**
Rose Sauvage Champagne, France NV   **$50   97**

This is undoubtedly the best-for-the-money rose on
the market. It smells and tastes like snappy, savory
and smoky red Burgundy, but with the cooling
refreshment of bubbles. The red cherry, floral potpourri and Asian spice notes simply sing out of the
glass, and the finish is endless. Pair it with teriyaki,
5-spice duck or chocolatey Mexican mole poblano.
Kitchen Survivor™ Grade: A+
Your notes: _____

Pierre Gimonnet 1er Cru Brut   **Pts**
Champagne, France NV   **$50   91**

Like lemon mousse minus the fat and sugar! Lacy
and vivacious on the palate, with ginger and green tea
notes. Sleek, long, perfect with eggs Benedict.
Kitchen Survivor™ Grade: A+
Your notes: _____

Pol Roger Extra Cuvee de Reserve   **Pts**
'Pure', Champagne, France NV   **$40   91**

One of the top brut Champagnes in the delicate style
with fragrant talcum, fresh cream and ripe pear notes,
perfectly proportioned and full of finesse. Pair with
mushroom risotto, lobster consomme or crab salad.
Kitchen Survivor™ Grade: A+
Your notes: _____

Taittinger (*TATE-in-jur*) Brut La   **Pts**
Française Champagne, France NV   **$45   92**

One of my favorites for its bewitching notes of fresh
fennel and Asian pear, and positively sleek texture.
Pair it with satiny scallops or oyster stew.
Kitchen Survivor™ Grade: A
Your notes: _____

TOP TEN FRENCH CHAMPAGNES: OVER $50

Bollinger (*BOLL-en-jur*) Brut Special   **Pts**
Cuvee Champagne, France NV   **$60**   **90**

Bollinger's alluring nutty-toasty, brioche scents and flavors and long finish make it a standout Brut NV.
Kitchen Survivor™ Grade: A
Your notes: _____

Charles Heidsieck (*HIDE-sick*) Brut   **Pts**
Reserve Champagne, France NV   **$55**   **98**

Simply breathtaking, with full-bodied toasted hazelnut and apple streusel flavors, and a long toffee finish. The depth, luxuriant texture and length are near perfection. Pairing with aged Gouda takes it there.
Kitchen Survivor™ Grade: A
Your notes: _____

Dom Perignon Champagne Brut,   **Pts**
France 2002   **$165**   **96**

The reputation seduces, and the quality keeps you smitten! Apple compote, bread dough and fresh hay scents are the signature, with a pure core of pear and anise and a long finish. Pair with saffron-scented risotto or roasted pork with braised leeks and fennel.
Kitchen Survivor™ Grade: B+
Your notes: _____

G.H. Mumm de Cramant Blanc de Blancs,   **Pts**
Champagne, France NV   **$55**   **93**

Cramant refers to a top "cru" (growing area) in Champagne where Chardonnay is planted - hence this specialty Blanc de Blancs. It is pure chamomile-and-potpourri elegance and finesse, but with a baked apple and toffee richness that sneaks up on you.
Kitchen Survivor™ Grade: A+
Your notes: _____

Krug Grande Cuvee Multivintage   **Pts**
Champagne, France   **$165**   **96**

I love this wine! Krug's truly unique mouth-filling, nutty, baked-brioche style is big enough to pair with roasted meats and game birds, or truffled risotto.
Kitchen Survivor™ Grade: A+
Your notes: _____

Perrier-Jouët (*PEAR-ee-ay JHWETT*) **Pts**
Fleur de Champagne Brut, France 2002 **$139** **94**
Elegant notes of white flowers, ladyfingers and apple tart dance delicately on the palate, and linger with an apple compote and crusty bread note in the finish.
Kitchen Survivor™ Grade: A
Your notes: _____

Piper-Heidsieck (*HIDE-sick*) Cuvee Brut **Pts**
2002 Champagne, France NV **$65** **93**
A fantastic example of a vintage Champagne, showing brioche, toffee and marzipan scents and flavors. Pair it with trout (or other fish) amandine, duck confit or smoked poultry with a nutty stuffing.
Kitchen Survivor™ Grade: A
Your notes: _____

Ruinart (*roo-ee-NAHR*) Blanc de Blancs **Pts**
Brut Champagne, France NV **$70** **91**
I adore blanc de blancs (made from 100% Chardonnay), and this is one of the classic producers. The scents of fresh cream and biscuits and lacy-racy acidity make it great with brunch fare--smoked salmon, eggs Benedict or a goat cheese omelet.
Kitchen Survivor™ Grade: A
Your notes: _____

Taittinger Comtes de Champagne Blanc **Pts**
de Blancs Champagne, France 1999 **$190** **96**
I love the like-no-other style: pure elegance, with toasty brioche & caramelized pear flavors, and a finish that lasts for days. Delicious with oysters roasted with butter, Pernod and cream, or eggs Benedict.
Kitchen Survivor™ Grade: A
Your notes: _____

Veuve Clicquot Brut Rose **Pts**
Champagne, France 2004 **$75** **97**
The iconic yellow label is Clicquot's calling card, but I adore the rose. This one is resplendent, with a texture that is at once sprightly and luscious. Complex notes of saffron, consomme, red currant and Asian spice are born to pair with Moroccan flavors or holiday turkey. Cellars beautifully - if you can wait!
Kitchen Survivor™ Grade: A
Your notes: _____

WHITE WINES

Pinot Gris &/Pinot Grigio

Grape Profile: Pinot Gris (*pee-no GREE*) is the French and Grigio (*GREE-jee-oh*) the Italian spelling for this white grape with a split personality. The French and American versions tend toward the luscious style. The Italian versions (and a few American imitators) are more mineral and crisp - mostly everyday drinking wines, although a few producers' bottlings stand above the pack and make truly special versions. It's worth trading up to them versus the under-$10 Italian PGs, most of which are at best watery and at worst, bitter - only one made my Top Ten! In France, Pinot Gris is a signature in the Alsace region, and Oregon vintners in particular have made this style a calling card (though they can be expensive for the quality). The California bottlings tend to be labeled according to the style they are mimicking - Pinot Gris if it's the exotic French style, Pinot Grigio if it's the crisp and minerally Italian style. To many it's the quintessential quaffing wine and an easy by the glass choice in restaurants. Happily, it remains true that you need not pay a lot for tasty Pinot Grigio/Gris. The choice is yours!

Serve: Well chilled; young and fresh (as one of my wine buying buddies says to the waiters *she* teaches: "The best vintage for Pinot Grigio? As close to yesterday as possible!").

When: Anytime, but ideal with cocktails, outdoor occasions, lunch, big gatherings (a crowd pleaser).

With: Very versatile, but perfect with hors d'oeuvres, salads, salty foods, and fried foods.

In: The One™ glass for white, or an all-purpose wineglass.

Almost Top Ten Pinot Gris/Grigios:

These wines are also well worth checking out.
(You can find my tasting notes at AndreaWine.com):

Adelsheim
Castello Banfi San Angelo
Danzante
Estancia
J Vineyards & Winery
Maso Canali
Ponzi
Pierre Sparr
Willamette Valley Vineyards

"Worth the splurge" Alsace Pinot Gris:

Weinbach
Trimbach Reserve Personnelle
Zind-Humbrecht

TOP TEN PINOT GRIS/GRIGIOS

Alois Lageder (ah-lo-EEZ *la-GAY-der*)   **Pts**
Pinot Grigio, Alto Adige, Italy 2009   **$18**   **89**

What classic Pinot Grigio is supposed to be: pear fruit, floral scent, and a snappy mineral finish tailor-made for pairing with clam pasta or salumi.

Kitchen Survivor™ Grade: B

Your notes: _____

Attems Pinot Grigio,   **Pts**
Collio, Italy 2009   **$16**   **93**

Such quality in a Pinot Grigio is thrilling: Meyer lemon, wet gravel on the nose; an intense core of stone fruit (peach, apricot), succulent pear and citrus peel on the palate. An endless creamy, bitter almond finish. The snap of laser acidity beckons another sip.

Kitchen Survivor™ Grade: B

Your notes: _____

Bollini Pinot Grigio Trentino,   **Pts**
Trentino-Alto Adige, Italy 2009   **$13**   **92**

The bitter almond, mascarpone and fresh pear notes in this wine set it apart from the Italian PG pack. The chalky minerality and creamy mouthfeel make it a fantastic partner for a pristine plate of fresh oysters.

Kitchen Survivor™ Grade: B

Your notes: _____

Clos du Bois Pinot Grigio,   **Pts**
California 2008   **$12**   **87**

Among all the big-brand Cali PGs, this juicy mouthful is a standout for its melon and peach fruit. Tasty for sipping on its own, and great with weeknight fare: Tex-Mex, Chinese, Caesar salad, fish 'n chips...

Kitchen Survivor™ Grade: B

Your notes: _____

Cupcake Pinot Grigio,   **Pts**
Trentino, Italy 2009   **$8**   **87**

This newcomer puts most other value-priced Italian PGs to shame. It charms with juicy Fuji apple tutti-frutti flavors, but has a backbone of minerality that says "Italy" and "mangia" with everyday meals. Bravo!

Kitchen Survivor™ Grade: B

Your notes: _____

Hugel Pinot Gris "Classic,"   **Pts**
Alsace, France 2009   **$16**   **90**
Textbook Alsace Pinot Gris for a phenomenal price!
It's subtle but full of character - fresh tarragon, Asian
pear and candied pineapple notes, plus a wet stone
minerality. Pair with Asian fare, salty snacks, char-
cuterie, fresh salads or mild cheeses.
Kitchen Survivor™ Grade: B
Your notes: _____

King Estate Signature Collection Pinot   **Pts**
Gris, Oregon 2009   **$17**   **90**
The best OR Pinot Gris I have had in years! The
scent is honeyed Asian pears and fresh fennel with a
hint of waxiness. The juicy pear fruit and hint of ginger on the palate were a blast to pair with everything
from grilled shrimp to heirloom tomatoes and basil.
Kitchen Survivor™ Grade: B
Your notes: _____

Livio Felluga (*LIV-ee-oh fuh-LOO-*   **Pts**
***guh*) Map Label Pinot Grigio, Italy 2009**   **$18**   **89**
Italian Pinot Grigio as it should be: fragrant with hay
and tree fruit notes, crisp and lively. Pairs like no
tomorrow, but my favorites are clam pasta, salty
snacks and cheeses, salads, even artichokes.
Kitchen Survivor™ Grade: B
Your notes: _____

Pighin Pinot Grigio Grave,   **Pts**
Italy 2009   **$16**   **91**
Pighin's 2009 is once again a truly great PG, showing
white flowers, grapefruit, minerals, ginger and fresh
pears. It's got super acidity, and a creamy anise note
that cries out for chilled bivalves or fennel salad.
Kitchen Survivor™ Grade: A
Your notes: _____

Woodbridge (Robert Mondavi)   **Pts**
Pinot Grigio, California 2009   **$8**   **87**
THE best bargain Pinot Grigio - crisp and chalky,
with zippy lemon notes and a long finish (when do
you say *that* about an under-$10 wine?). Sip solo, or
pair with salads, garlicky pastas, any form of takeout.
Kitchen Survivor™ Grade: B
Your notes: _____

Riesling

Grape Profile: I am thrilled to say that after many years of steering clear, consumers have finally embraced Riesling, one of my very favorite grapes. There's lots to love, including the price/quality ratio, and high Kitchen Survivor™ grades - thanks to their tangy, crisp acidity, Riesling wines really hold up in the fridge. That makes them ideal for lots of everyday dining situations, e.g., you want a glass of white with your takeout sushi, but your dinner mate wants red with the beef teriyaki. Or maybe you want to start with a glass of white wine while you're cooking dinner and then switch to red with the meal. It's nice to know that with many Rieslings you can go back to the wine over several days, and every glass will taste as good as the first one.

Germany, the traditional source of great Rieslings, continues to grow its presence in the *Guide*. And that's great, because no other region offers so many *world class* wines for under $30. Look for German Rieslings from the Mosel, Rheingau, Pfalz, and Nahe regions. Other go-to Riesling regions are Austria, Alsace in France, and Washington.

Prepare to be impressed. Rieslings are generally light bodied but loaded with stunning fruit flavor, balanced with tangy acidity. Take note of the value bottlings for delicious crowd-pleasing drinking. The classic producers listed here (from Alsace, Germany, Austria and the United States) set the standard for Riesling, and are worshipped by sommeliers for how their wines pair and age. If you can't find the particular bottling I've noted here, you can be confident buying any Riesling they make. They are specialists with the utmost pedigree.

Serve: Lightly chilled is fine (the aromas really shine when it's not ice cold); it's good young and fresh, but the French and German versions can evolve nicely anywhere from 5-30 years.

When: Every day (okay, my personal taste there); classy enough for "important" meals and occasions.

With: Outstanding with shellfish and ethnic foods with a "kick" (think Asian, Thai, Indian, Mexican). There's also an awesome rule-breaker match: braised meats and BBQ!

In: The One™ glass for white, or an all-purpose wineglass.

Almost Top Ten Rieslings:

These wines are also well worth checking out:
Argyle
Dashe
Gunderloch
Mirassou
Wolf Blass
Grosset
Penfolds
Willi Schaefer

"Worth the splurge" Rieslings:

Weinbach, Alsace
Trimbach Clos Ste. Hune, Alsace
Zind-Humbrecht, Alsace
Prager Achleiten Stockkultur, Austria

"Dr. L" Loosen Brothers Riesling,   Pts
Mosel, Germany 2009 $12   88

Textbook Mosel: peaches 'n' cream, slaty minerality, a tender sense of sweetness like a ripe tangerine. Pair with clam and sausage pasta or spicy Tex Mex.

Kitchen Survivor™ Grade: A

Your notes: _____

Dr. Loosen Estate Riesling Kabinett Blue   Pts
Slate, Mosel, Germany 2009 $23   90

Blue Slate refers to the soil, which comes through in the petrol scent. Soft and creamy, with pure pleasure-notes of peach yogurt and fresh apples. Pair with spicy takeout, smoky salumi, or gooey cheese.

Kitchen Survivor™ Grade: A

Your notes: _____

Leitz Dragonstone Riesling,   Pts
Rheingau, Germany 2009 $18   91

Incredible - fleshy Mandarin orange fruit without a lot of weight, and a whisper of sweet tarragon and red currant. The touch of sweetness will cut through spicy heat - think crab boil or Buffalo wings.

Kitchen Survivor™ Grade: A

Your notes: _____

Leitz Eins Zwei Dry Riesling,   Pts
Rheingau, Germany 2009 $16   92

Figures a great producer like Leitz could put out a real-deal German dry Riesling for a song. Take in every detail of the gingery-tangerine-flowers-and-buttermilk fragrance and flavor, then just kick back and enjoy with anything from a BLT to eggs Benedict.

Kitchen Survivor™ Grade: A+

Your notes: _____

Markus Molitor Haus Klosterberg Riesling   Pts
Dry, Mosel, Germany 2009 $16   91

Lemon cream, quince preserves, delicate peach and white flowers all scream "drink me." Amazingly long on the finish for such a value-priced wine.
Pair it with steamed mussels and clams or spicy sushi.

Kitchen Survivor™ Grade: A

Your notes: _____

Meulenhof Erdener Treppchen Riesling   **Pts**
Spatlese Old Vines, Mosel, Germany 2009   **$19**   **94**

Honeysuckle & vanilla cream. If the mango fruit weren't so luscious you'd want to dab it behind your earlobes before a date! Pairing it with spicy sushi, Indian curries or Thai food will be just as seductive.

Kitchen Survivor™ Grade: A

Your notes: _____

Prinz von Hessen Riesling,   **Pts**
Rheingau, Germany 2008   **$15**   **90**

The trifecta: affordable, amazingly yummy, authentic. The ginger-and-saffron savoriness along with grapefruit, quince, tangerine and crisp apple notes make quite a statement. Right at home anywhere, from a BBQ with the boys to a ladies' lunch!

Kitchen Survivor™ Grade: A+

Your notes: _____

Robert Weil Estate Riesling   **Pts**
Trocken, Rheingau, Germany 2009   **$28**   **93**

A stunning neon tangerine fruit and rosehips wine, with an endless fruit-and-minerals finish. Dreamy with creamy cheese such as burrata or Camembert.

Kitchen Survivor™ Grade: A+

Your notes: _____

Saint M Riesling, Pfalz,   **Pts**
Germany 2009   **$12**   **90**

What a combo - the low price and succulent peaches-and-cream taste and scent will have you hooked on German Riesling in no time (all a part of my master plan!).

Kitchen Survivor™ Grade: A+

Your notes: _____

Selbach-Oster Zeltinger Schlossberg   **Pts**
Riesling Spatlese, Mosel, Germany 2009   **$30**   **94**

A soft honeyed, mushroomy minerality underpins softly racy-spicy, creamy apricot and ginger flavors. My "wow" pairing? Spicy dry-rubbed BBQ ribs.

Kitchen Survivor™ Grade: A+

Your notes: _____

TOP TEN RIESLINGS:
ALSACE & AUSTRIA

Brundlmayer Riesling Heiligenstein Alte   **Pts**
Reben, Kamptal, Austria 2008   **$50**   **94**

One of the world's great wines, with an alluring creaminess that's unique to Austrian Rieslings. The gorgeous quince, melon, ginger, wet rocks and warm hay notes are stamps of the Heiligenstein. Ages great, and Mr. Brundlmayer pairs it with Thai food.
Kitchen Survivor™ Grade: A
Your notes: _____

Emmerich Knoll Riesling Smaragd,   **Pts**
Wachau, Austria 2008   **$36**   **92**

The exotic flowers, tangerine and ripe stone fruits in the scent echo on the creamy palate and into the smoky finish. Pair with Asian fare or smoked pork or duck.
Kitchen Survivor™ Grade: A
Your notes: _____

Hirsch Zobinger Heiligenstein Riesling,   **Pts**
Kamptal, Austria 2008   **$36**   **92**

The sweet quince, kumquat and Asian pear scents and flavors charm, but the smoky minerality and fromage blanc creaminess on the palate and finish are classic to this terroir. A great match for Thai and Indian curries.
Kitchen Survivor™ Grade: A
Your notes: _____

Domaine Weinbach Riesling Grand Cru,   **Pts**
Schlossberg, Alsace 2008   **$48**   **97**

One of the most amazing white wines, ever. The neon flavors of ripe apple, candied lemon peel, passion fruit and white peach are enlivened by an amazing zing of acidity and talc minerality. The finish is endless. For an unforgettable Thanksgiving, invite this wine to dinner!
Kitchen Survivor™ Grade: A
Your notes: _____

Hugel Riesling Jubilee,   **Pts**
Alsace, France 2005   **$30**   **94**

This wine's stony minerality, lush Asian pear and peach fruit, tender texture and incredible length blew me away. Proof positive that real depth in a white is not

about oak, it's about the soil. Pair with smoked pork, hot-smoked salmon or steamed mussels.
Kitchen Survivor™ Grade: A
Your notes: _____

Pierre Sparr Selection Riesling, Alsace, France 2008

Pts $9   90

Beaucoup charm for the price. Tangerine, crisp apple and just a touch of sweetness make it great for sipping solo, or with spicy foods such as Thai or Indian. Bravo!
Kitchen Survivor™ Grade: A
Your notes: _____

Prager Wachstum Bodenstein Riesling Smaragd, Wachau, Austria 2008

Pts $38   94

Sleek and elegant with crisp pear, talcum, lemon and chamomile scents and flavors, a steely minerality and long, fragrant finish. Pair with creamy oyster stew.
Kitchen Survivor™ Grade: A
Your notes: _____

Trimbach Riesling, Alsace, France 2008

Pts $18   91

A benchmark that's bone-dry, with scents of chalk, hay and flowers, green apple and limoncello fruit, and not a whiff of oak. Great with lemon-buttery trout.
Kitchen Survivor™ Grade: A+
Your notes: _____

Trimbach Riesling Cuvee Frederic Emile, Alsace 2005

Pts $36   94

This wine is always released with bottle age and will improve for decades more. That said, the buttermilk, wet stone and lemon yogurt notes on the palate and finish give great pleasure now, especially with shellfish.
Kitchen Survivor™ Grade: A
Your notes: _____

Zind-Humbrecht Riesling "Zind" Alsace 2008

Pts $20   91

This intro wine is the key that unlocks the secret ZH wine garden: all stone fruit and persimmon lushness with chamomile and waxy notes. Olivier Humbrecht's wines are so seductive most people get lost forever in that wine garden - come join us!
Kitchen Survivor™ Grade: B+
Your notes: _____

TOP TEN RIESLINGS: NEW WORLD

Barnard-Griffin Riesling, Columbia Valley,   **Pts**
Washington 2009   **$11**   **90**

Another superb value Riesling from Washington, this one for lovers of the tropical, passion fruit style. Invite this one to lunch or dinner and that'll be you!

Kitchen Survivor™ Grade: B

Your notes: _____

Chateau Ste. Michelle Dry Riesling,   **Pts**
Columbia Valley, Washington 2009   **$14**   **89**

A classic American Riesling with new world-style pineapple sundae flavors, great concentration and a lovely tangerine finish. Delicious with rich pates and spicy Asian and Tex-Mex fare.

Kitchen Survivor™ Grade: B

Your notes: _____

Eroica (*ee-ROY-cuh*) Riesling, Columbia   **Pts**
Valley, Washington 2009   **$22**   **94**

Still America's best Riesling, with a laser purity of tangerine, quince and starfruit, along with a delicate slaty minerality. Delicious young with crab, shellfish & spicy fare, but put some aside for five years for a yummy twist - with age it becomes creamy and nutty.

Kitchen Survivor™ Grade: A+

Your notes: _____

Kendall-Jackson Vintner's Reserve   **Pts**
Riesling, Monterey, California 2009   **$12**   **89**

If you're new to Riesling, try this one for a blue chip brand name & lovely varietal character - honeysuckle & white peach with allspice and a whisper of sweetness. A home run with Thai or Chinese food.

Kitchen Survivor™ Grade: A

Your notes: _____

Jacob's Creek Reserve Riesling,   **Pts**
South Australia 2009   **$14**   **90**

Dry, delicious and true to the grape for a great price- what more do you want? There's a nice gingery-white pepper savor alongside juicy citrus, crisp apple and tarragon notes. Pair with smoked meats or shellfish.

Kitchen Survivor™ Grade: B

Your notes: _____

Pacific Rim Dry Riesling,   Pts
USA/Germany 2009   **$14**   90

This endures as a benchmark for value and character thanks to its succulent peaches-and-cream style. *Pacific Rim* is the winery's shorthand for "drink with Asian foods" like sushi, Thai or Chinese.

Kitchen Survivor™ Grade: A

Your notes: _____

Robert Mondavi Private Selection   Pts
Riesling, California 2009   **$15**   88

The tangerine with a touch of petrol and peach classic Riesling, and the pairability and price point make this "house wine" and "party wine" material.

Kitchen Survivor™ Grade: B+

Your notes: _____

Smith-Madrone Riesling,   Pts
Napa, California 2009   **$27**   90

One of America's top Rieslings, impressive for its complex notes of peach yogurt, melon, petrol and chamomile. A great match for sweet crab or shrimp.

Kitchen Survivor™ Grade: A

Your notes: _____

Snoqualmie 'Naked' Riesling, Columbia   Pts
Valley, Washington 2009   **$10**   88

Tastes great, feels great: redolent with white peach, zippy lemon curd and cream flavors, *and* made from organically grown grapes!

Kitchen Survivor™ Grade: A

Your notes: _____

Trefethen Estate Dry Riesling,   Pts
Napa 2009   **$22**   92

A benchmark American Riesling, with lovely grapefruit-lime flavors and a mineral tang - perfect for pairing with classic fish dishes - crab Louis, trout amandine, oysters on the half shell.

Kitchen Survivor™ Grade: A

Your notes: _____

Sauvignon Blanc/Fumé Blanc

Grape Profile: Sauvignon Blanc (*soh-veen-yoan BLAHNK*), one of my favorite white wine grapes, is one of the most exciting right now for consumers for two reasons. First, truly great ones are still available for under $15—something you can't say about many wine categories these days. Second, when you trade up in price just a little, the rewards in complexity and character can be breathtaking. So SB, along with Riesling, are great grapes to explore in-depth when you are looking to try new and different wines without spending a fortune. Depending on where SB is grown (cool, moderate, or warm zones), the exotically pungent scent and taste range from zesty and herbal to tangy lime-grapefruit to juicy peach and melon, to tropical fruit and figs, with vibrant acidity. Although the grape's home base is France's Loire Valley and Bordeaux regions, switching to a Top-Ten focus forced me to face up to an unfortunate fact: other countries' offerings are out-doing the French classics from the Loire Valley and Bordeaux, especially in terms of value for the money. My recommendations here are some of the better bottlings that remain fairly available and affordable. When you try these, you will see that the Loire Valley versions are classically minerally, with elegance and great acidity; the Bordeaux versions are most often barrel-fermented and blended with the local Semillon grape, giving them a waxy, creamy richness. California and Washington State make excellent versions, often labeled Fumé Blanc (*FOO-may BLAHNK*) - a tip-off that the wine is barrel-fermented and barrel-aged, and thus fuller in body. In the Southern Hemisphere, New Zealand Sauvignon Blancs continue to earn pro and consumer raves, South Africa produces some smokin' examples, and now Chile is coming on strong with great bottlings that scream character for a bargain price. Another of Sauvignon Blanc's major virtues is its food versatility: It goes so well with the foods many people eat regularly (especially those following a less-red-meat regimen), like chicken and turkey, salads, sushi, Mexican, and vegetarian. I also recently discovered, as I was working more of the really-good-for-you foods into my diet, that SB is a great match for many of them - namely, broccoli and other cruciferous veggies, avocados, olive oil and of course, tomatoes!

> **THANKS, KIWIS!** Most New Zealand Sauvignon Blancs are now bottled with a screw cap for your convenience and to ensure you get fresh wine without "corkiness" (see "Buying Lingo" for a definition). Hooray!

Serve: Chilled but not ice cold.

When: An amazing food partner, but the tasting notes also spotlight styles that are good on their own, as an aperitif.

With: As noted, great with most everyday eats as well as popular ethnic tastes like Mexican food.

In: The One™ glass for white, or an all-purpose wineglass.

Almost Top Ten Sauvignon Blanc/Fumé Blancs:

The following wines are also well worth checking out:

Mason
Voss
Kathryn Hall
Selene
Chateau Rahoul
Chateau Coucheroy
Concha y Toro Terrunyo
Cakebread
Murphy-Goode
Thelema
Drylands
Longboat
Tement
Murrieta's Well Meritage

TOP TEN SAUVIGNON BLANCS: NEW WORLD $15 OR LESS

Brancott Sauvignon Blanc,   **Pts**
Marlborough, New Zealand 2009   **$11**   **89**

A perennial NZ SB value, with all the classic character: cut grass, gooseberry, grapefruit and passion fruit and a flinty finish. Bring on the guacamole!
Kitchen Survivor™ Grade: A

Your notes: _____

Casa Lapostolle (*lah-poh-STOLE*)   **Pts**
Sauvignon Blanc, Casablanca, Chile 2009   **$10**   **89**

As always, a value star, with crisp green apple and fresh peach flavors. Pair with ceviche or green salads.
Kitchen Survivor™ Grade: B

Your notes: _____

Chateau Ste. Michelle Horse Heaven Hills   **Pts**
Sauvignon Blanc, Washington 2009   **$14**   **90**

You get so much tropical fruit, ginger and tangerine character for the money, why not splurge and partner it with fresh crab or peel 'n' eat shrimp?
Kitchen Survivor™ Grade: B

Your notes: _____

Dry Creek Vineyard Fumé Blanc,   **Pts**
Sonoma, California 2009   **$12**   **89**

At once lively and creamy, this is a yummy yin-yang of citrus and white peach that's delicious on its own but also a great partner for salads and smoked salmon.
Kitchen Survivor™ Grade: A

Your notes: _____

Joel Gott Sauvignon Blanc,   **Pts**
California 2009   **$10**   **89**

Always a fruit salad-in-a-glass crowd-pleaser, lush with kiwi and ripe apple fruit, kissed with a snap of citrus acidity. Great value, great match for Tex Mex!
Kitchen Survivor™ Grade: A+

Your notes:: _____

Kendall-Jackson Vintner's Reserve   **Pts**
Sauvignon Blanc, California 2008   **$12**   **89**

When luscious tropical meets lively citrus, you have CA SB at its best, as in this bottling, which makes me crave BBQ'd oysters or a garlicky fish chowder.
Kitchen Survivor™ Grade: A
Your notes: _____

Nobilo Regional Collection Sauvignon   **Pts**
Blanc, Marlborough, New Zealand 2009   **$10**   **89**

Skip the margaritas and serve this zippy, savory-flinty lime and crisp apple glassful with Mexican food. But don't stop there-it's incredibly versatile with salads, seafoods, cheeses, smoked meats and brunch fare.
Kitchen Survivor™ Grade: A
Your notes: _____

Veramonte Sauvignon Blanc,   **Pts**
Chile 2009   **$12**   **90**

One of Chile's top SBs is also one of its best value wines, with exotic kiwi, honeydew, and passion fruit flavors and a super-long finish. Pair with fish tacos or Gouda cheese and mushroom quesadillas.
Kitchen Survivor™ Grade: B
Your notes: _____

Wente Louis Mel Sauvignon Blanc,   **Pts**
Livermore, California 2009   **$11**   **90**

An amazing wine for the money - dripping with honeydew, key lime, passion fruit and white peach flavors and scents. Tasty on its own and delicious with goat cheese or heirloom tomatoes in a salad or BLT.
Kitchen Survivor™ Grade: A
Your notes: _____

Woodbridge Sauvignon Blanc,   **Pts**
California 2009   **$6**   **88**

You can't find better SB in this price point. Arguably you can't find better *white wine* at this price point. There's plenty of snappy, grassy-citrus varietal character, soft melon on the palate, and great food affinity for guacamole, ceviche, salads. Pick up a case!
Kitchen Survivor™ Grade: B
Your notes: _____

TOP TEN SAUVIGNON BLANCS: NEW WORLD $15 - $25

Cliff Lede Sauvignon Blanc,   **Pts**
Napa, California 2009   **$20**   **93**

It's worth the search for this special wine, redolent of tender peach fruit but with loads of flinty, grapefruit liveliness that make it unbeatable with fresh tomato salads or garlicky seafood stews & pastas.

Kitchen Survivor™ Grade: A

Your notes: _____

Benziger Sauvignon Blanc,   **Pts**
Sonoma, California 2009   **$16**   **89**

Lively buttermilk, Meyer lemon, fresh pear and chalky notes, plus a creaminess from light oak aging, make this a perfect partner for fresh goat cheese.

Kitchen Survivor™ Grade: A

Your notes: _____

Frog's Leap Sauvignon Blanc,   **Pts**
Rutherford, Napa, California 2009   **$18**   **90**

The 100% SB character of gooseberries and flinty, penetrating citrus is always utterly delicious (not just leap years!). Super with beet and goat cheese salad.

Kitchen Survivor™ Grade: A

Your notes: _____

Girard Sauvignon Blanc,   **Pts**
Rutherford, Napa, California 2009   **$16**   **NA**

Fresh melon fruit with a hint of grapefruit and exotic lychee perfume. I can't give it a score because my vineyard's grapes go into this wine, but I do recommend it! Delicious with Camembert quesadillas.

Kitchen Survivor™ Grade: A

Your notes: _____

Matanzas Creek Sauvignon Blanc,   **Pts**
Sonoma, California 2007   **$24**   **92**

I have put this classy, blue chip SB on wine lists for years, and it always delivers great melon-peach fruit and creamy texture- like a Chard but with crisper acidity. A great match for lobster or scallops.

Kitchen Survivor™ Grade: A+

Your notes: _____

Morgan Sauvignon Blanc, Monterey, Pts
California 2009 $16 90

The Monterey sun gives a tropical pineapple ripeness, tempered with tangy lime acidity thanks to the
cool bay breezes. Delicious on its own, but also super
easy to pair, with anything from garlic to wasabi.
Kitchen Survivor™ Grade: A
Your notes: _____

Mulderbosch Sauvignon Blanc, Pts
Stellenbosch, South Africa 2009 $17 92

There is nothing quite like it: scents of flint, cream,
avocados, olive oil and key lime so complex it makes
your head spin; delicious kiwi and green apple fruit
on the palate; incredibly looong finish.
Kitchen Survivor™ Grade: A
Your notes: _____

Robert Mondavi Napa Fumé Blanc, Pts
Napa, California 2008 $20 94

Perennially one of America's best whites, this often
wins in my blind tastings against much pricier bottles. It's got fig fruit, lemon thyme honeyed beeswax
notes, with a rich creamy texture that's a stellar
match for goat cheese quesadillas with guacamole.
Kitchen Survivor™ Grade: B+
Your notes: _____

St. Supery Sauvignon Blanc, Napa, Pts
California 2009 $23 93

I chose this standout SB for Delta because I know the
exotic fennel, fig and grilled pineapple notes, and the
citrus tanginess, will shine at altitude and pair great
with anything from salad to pasta to smoked salmon.
Kitchen Survivor™ Grade: A+
Your notes: _____

Silverado Miller Ranch Sauvignon Blanc, Pts
Napa, California 2009 $22 94

Free of oak, and chock-full of laser-pure fruit: melon,
apple, peach and passion fruit, all layered and linger-
ing into the endless finish. One of the best Cali SBs,
period. Pair with clams or steamed mussels.
Kitchen Survivor™ Grade: A
Your notes _____

TOP TEN SAUVIGNON BLANCS: NEW WORLD $25 & UP

Araujo Eisele Vineyard Sauvignon Blanc,   **Pts**
Napa Valley, California 2009   **$40**   **95**
Vivid layers of papaya and guava with a tangerine tang that keeps you yearning for more. One of the best SBs in all of California and worth the splurge.
Kitchen Survivor™ Grade: A
Your notes: _____

Chalk Hill Winery Sauvignon Blanc,   **Pts**
Chalk Hill-Sonoma, California 2008   **$28**   **95**
Opulent without being over-the-top. The lavish oak imparts a vanilla-creaminess to the succulent grilled pineapple and honey flavors. Bring on the lobster!
Kitchen Survivor™ Grade: B+
Your notes: _____

Delille Cellars Chaleur Estate Blanc   **Pts**
Columbia Valley, Washington 2009   **$34**   **94**
Collectors should seek this one out for the cellar - it ages beautifully for 5-7 years, at least. Made in the Bordeaux style with barrel fermentation and some Semillon in the blend, it is creamy, toasty, and full, with opulent but balanced buttercream and pineapple on the palate. Pair it decadently: truffle risotto!
Kitchen Survivor™ Grade: A+
Your notes: _____

Duckhorn Sauvignon Blanc, Napa   **Pts**
California 2009   **$25**   **90**
The signature tangerine-green apple, fruit kissed with a touch of waxy creaminess from partial barrel fermentation, are this blue chip SB's signature. Pair with sundried tomato and goat cheese pasta.
Kitchen Survivor™ Grade: A
Your notes: _____

Flora Springs Soliloquy, Napa,   **Pts**
California 2009   **$25**   **92**
I love the laser-pure key lime and kiwi fruit, steely minerality and tingly acidity of this vibrant wine that's tailor-made for fried green tomatoes.
Kitchen Survivor™ Grade: A+
Your notes: _____

Grgich (*GER-gich;* both are hard   **Pts**
***g* as in *girl*) Hills Fumé Blanc,**   **$28**   **94**
Napa Valley, California 2009

One of the best SBs I have had all year. Incredibly exotic notes of tangy passion fruit, honeydew melon, papaya, lemongrass and coconut milk. Pair with curried shrimp or Brie quesadillas with guacamole.

Kitchen Survivor™ Grade: A+

Your notes: _____

Merry Edwards Sauvignon Blanc, Russian   **Pts**
River Valley, California 2009   **$30**   **95**

An absolutely heady wine, well worth the search and the splurge. Explosive passion fruit, lemongrass and compoted nectarine flavors are wrapped in a textured palate that is both creamy and zingy - how'd they do that? Pair it with fish tacos with guacamole and aioli.

Kitchen Survivor™ Grade: A+

Your notes: _____

Robert Mondavi To-Ka-Lon Reserve   **Pts**
Fumé Blanc, Napa, California 2008   **$40**   **94**

Toasty, creamy, waxy and honeyed, with a core of lemon pie and pineapple flavors. Caramelized leeks, or a Hollandaise dish, are blow-you-away pairings.

Kitchen Survivor™ Grade: B+

Your notes: _____

Spottswoode Sauvignon Blanc, Napa,   **Pts**
California 2009   **$35**   **90**

Elegant and flinty, with notes of hay and fresh-cut grass. The palate is laser-pure green papaya, pineapple and tangy kiwi fruit. Serve with warm goat cheese salad, scallop ceviche or dill-cured salmon.

Kitchen Survivor™ Grade: A+

Your notes: _____

Rochioli Sauvignon Blanc, Russian   **Pts**
River Valley, California 2009   **$39**   **94**

Elegant and exotic golden pineapple, Asian pear and sweet gardenia fragrance, succulent white peach on the palate--pair with seared scallops in citrus butter.

Kitchen Survivor™ Grade: A+

Your notes: _____

TOP TEN SAUVIGNON BLANCS: OLD WORLD & NEW ZEALAND

Brancott Reserve Sauvignon Blanc, **Pts**
Marlborough, New Zealand 2009 **$18** **91**
A great NZ SBs, packed with the "3Gs": grapefruit, grass and gooseberry. Pair it with another "g," goat cheese (or guacamole!), to unleash the passion fruit!
Kitchen Survivor™ Grade: A+
Your notes: _____

Cloudy Bay Sauvignon Blanc, **Pts**
Marlborough, New Zealand 2009 **$26** **90**
The wine whose "grassy gooseberry" style put NZ SB on the map has evolved. Riper pineapple fruit and a new buttermilky creamy texture notches it up. The classic match is mussels steamed in coconut milk!
Kitchen Survivor™ Grade: B+
Your notes: _____

Cloudy Bay Te Koko Sauvignon Blanc, **Pts**
Marlborough, New Zealand 2006 **$55** **92**
Not your typical NZ SB: wildly exotic kiwi, honeydew, honey, mushrooms and cheesecake scents and flavors are like silk and neon on the palate. Pair with fine, mild cheeses or seared scallops in beurre blanc.
Kitchen Survivor™ Grade: B
Your notes: _____

Chateau Carbonnieux Blanc, Pessac- **Pts**
Leognan, Bordeaux, France 2007 **$34** **89**
The classic wet gravel, grapefruit and fresh apple notes softened with hints of fresh cream make this wine the perfect partner for subtle sauteed fin fish such as sole or trout with a lemon cream sauce.
Kitchen Survivor™ Grade: A+
Your notes: _____

Chateau de Sancerre Sancerre, **Pts**
Loire Valley, France 2008 **$19** **89**
This is a superb example of the racy chamomile-and-apples style of Sancerre. On the palate it is zippy with more fresh apple flavor, but then finishes long and nutty - the perfect match for trout amandine.
Kitchen Survivor™ Grade: A
Your notes: _____

Chateau Loudenne Blanc,   **Pts**
Bordeaux, France 2007   **$20**   **90**

A top value white Bordeaux, full of character and food versatility. Chalky citrus and apple scents lead to ripe pear and a waxy, creamy note from the 40% Semillon in the mix. Pair with a buttery leek gratin.

Kitchen Survivor™ Grade: B

Your notes: _____

Jolivet (Pascal) Sancerre, (*jhoe-lee-VAY*   **Pts**
***sahn-SAIR*), Loire Valley, France 2008**   **$22**   **89**

A major favorite of sommeliers, this creamy-chalky, citrusy, utterly alive wine shows buttermilk, crisp apple, tarragon and gunflint notes. A classic match for goat cheese or oysters on the half shell.

Kitchen Survivor™ Grade: A+

Your notes: _____

Kim Crawford Sauvignon Blanc,   **Pts**
Marlborough, New Zealand 2009   **$19**   **89**

This is a benchmark for what I consider to be the "new-style" NZ SB - a pure expression passion fruit and grapefruit rather than gooseberry and herbs. That makes it a lovely match for Asian fare.

Kitchen Survivor™ Grade: B

Your notes: _____

Pastou Sancerre Les Boucaults,   **Pts**
Loire Valley, France 2009   **$17**   **92**

One of the best, and best-value, Sancerres on the market, year after year, with sleek and refreshing notes of lime, fresh hay, lemon yogurt and minerals - perfect for fish baked with lemon and herbs.

Kitchen Survivor™ Grade: B+

Your notes: _____

Villa Maria Cellar Selection Sauvignon   **Pts**
Blanc, Marlborough 2009   **$18**   **89**

This is a top example of the ultra-herbaceous style of NZ SB. The scent is pungent with dill, green chile pepper, lime and grapefruit peel. On the palate, concentrated lime, dill and savory sundried tomato flavors scream for Cioppino, Caprese salad, tortilla soup, huevos rancheros...hungry?

Kitchen Survivor™ Grade: B

Your notes: _____

Chardonnay

Grape Profile: Chardonnay is the top-selling white varietal wine in this country and the fullest-bodied of the major white grapes. That rich body, along with Chardonnay's signature fruit intensity, could explain its extraordinary popularity with Americans, although in truth this grape's style is pretty chameleon-like. It can yield wines of legendary quality, ranging from crisp and austere to soft and juicy to utterly lush and exotic (and very often oaky), depending on whether it's grown in a cool, moderate, or warm climate. I am pleased to say that, based on the broad popularity of varying styles, including the growing "unoaked or "oak free" style, buyers find all of these styles worthy, perhaps offering some hope to pros who bemoan a noticeable "sameness" to many of the supermarket brand names. All Chardonnays are modeled on white Burgundy wines from France. The world-class versions are known for complexity, and often oakiness; the very best are age worthy. The rest, in the $25-and-under price tier, are pleasant styles meant for current drinking. Because most of the wines are made in very small quantities, I have focused my recommendations on the more affordable benchmarks that, with some searching, you should be able to find. California Chardonnays by far dominate store and restaurant sales, but the quality and value of both Washington State's and Australia's can be just as good. Although no Oregon offerings made the survey due to limited production, they're worth seeking out. Outside of Australia, Chardonnay is not a particular calling card of the Southern Hemisphere; I have included the worthy examples in this listing.

Serve: Chilled; however, extreme cold mutes the complexity of the top bottlings. Pull them off the ice if they get too cold.

When: There's no occasion where Chardonnay *isn't* welcomed by the majority of wine lovers; the grape's abundant fruit makes it great on its own, as an aperitif or a cocktail alternative.

With: Some sommeliers carp that Chardonnay "doesn't go well with food," but I don't think most consumers agree. Maybe they have a point that it "overpowers" some delicate culinary creations in luxury restaurants, but for those of us doing most of our eating and drinking in less-rarefied circumstances, it's a great partner for all kinds of food. The decadent, oaky/buttery styles that are California's calling card can even handle steak. And my personal favorite matches are lobster when I'm splurging, and buttered popcorn or aged Gouda cheese when I'm not. Any of these 3 pairings will make you swoon.

In: The One™ glass for white, or an all-purpose wineglass.

Almost Top Ten Chardonnays:

Steal
Blackstone Monterey
BV Coastal Estates
Robert Mondavi Private Selection

Moderate
Beringer Napa
Taz
Franciscan
Simi
Darcie Kent

Splurge
Robert Mondavi Reserve
Morgan Double L
Chateau Montelena
Cakebread

Emerging names

C. Donatiello
Inspiration
Stuhlmuller
Tandem
Three Sticks

Cellar No. 8 Chardonnay,   **Pts**
California 2008   **$11**   **90**

One of the best value Chards ever! It's exactly what
you want from California Chardonnay - juicy and
mouth-filling, with ripe apple fruit and a touch of cinnamon spice and vanilla from contact with oak. Delicious on its own and with anything from roast chicken
to grilled shrimp to Caesar salad. Pick up a case!
Kitchen Survivor™ Grade: B
Your notes: _____

Clos du Bois Chardonnay, North Coast,   **Pts**
California 2009   **$12**   **89**

A huge seller, for good reason: lots of crisp apple and
melon fruit with a subtle buttered popcorn scent—at
a good price. A great match with smoked chicken.
Kitchen Survivor™ Grade: B
Your notes: _____

Hess Select Chardonnay,   **Pts**
Monterey, California 2008   **$10**   **89**

Look up "Crowd Pleaser" in the wine dictionary, and
you might see this label, because the luscious and
lively mango, pear and lemony citrus notes along with
a soft kiss of vanilla oakiness, are irresistible.
Kitchen Survivor™ Grade: B
Your notes: _____

Jacob's Creek Reserve Chardonnay,   **Pts**
Australia 2009   **$12**   **90**

Tastes like baby Meursault - toasty, stony and a little
buttery, with concentrated pineapple, pear and baked
apple fruit and super-long finish. Pair with buttery
mushrooms, devilled crab or aged Gouda cheese.
Kitchen Survivor™ Grade: B
Your notes: _____

Lockwood Chardonnay, Monterey   **Pts**
California 2008   **$11**   **88**

The snappy Fuji and Golden Delicious apple flavor
with a kiss of vanilla make this a great sipper. Yet it's

so balanced it could handle all the flavors of Thanks-giving dinner (not to mention everyday dinner).
Kitchen Survivor™ Grade: B
Your notes: _____

Main Street Chardonnay, Santa Barbara County, California 2008

Pts $11 89

A truly yummy Chardonnay for a great price, with lots of tropical mango/papaya fruit that would pair beautifully with curry or Tex Mex fare.
Kitchen Survivor™ Grade: B
Your notes: _____

McWilliam's Hanwood Estate Chardonnay, Australia 2008

Pts $10 90

Always on my best-buy list because the fruit-salad-in-a-glass style is juicy and irresistible. Buy it by the case and pair with everything from grilled cheese to corn on the cob to pasta to chicken enchiladas.
Kitchen Survivor™ Grade: C
Your notes: _____

Penfolds Koonunga Hill Chardonnay, Australia 2009

Pts $12 89

Lots of Chard bang for the buck, with ripe apple fruit, spice and butterscotch, all in balance. Pair with grilled chicken Caesar, corn chowder or popcorn.
Kitchen Survivor™ Grade: B
Your notes: _____

Wolf Blass Yellow Label Chardonnay, Australia 2009

Pts $9 89

Such a cut above most other big-brand Aussie Chards at a similar price. It's got lively apple-peach-melon fruit, creamy texture and classy toasty oak.
Kitchen Survivor™ Grade: B
Your notes: _____

Woodbridge Chardonnay, California 2009

Pts $8 87

A budget Chard that delivers: soft apple compote fruit and a creamy texture and toastiness from light oak. Tasty on its own, and great with everyday dinners from Caesar salad to cheesy pasta, to leftovers!
Kitchen Survivor™ Grade: C
Your notes: _____

TOP TEN CHARDONNAYS: NEW WORLD $12-$20

Au Bon Climat Santa Barbara Chardonnay, California 2009   **$20**   **Pts 92**

Subtle oak and flamboyant guava and mango fruit are the signature of this wine that begs to be paired with Asian fusion and Tex-Mex fare. It's pure hedonistic pleasure, without being over the top.

Kitchen Survivor™ Grade: A

Your notes: _____

Calera Central Coast Chardonnay, California 2009   **$17**   **Pts 93**

More character and yum-factor than most CA chards at twice the price. Exuberant floral and tropical fruit notes steal the spotlight while a touch of spicy oakiness bats cleanup on the finish. A homerun with Thanksgiving turkey & trimmings.

Kitchen Survivor™ Grade: A+

Your notes: _____

Cambria Katherine's Vineyard Chardonnay, Santa Maria, California 2009   **$20**   **Pts 89**

This wine has lavish toasty oak and tropical fruit, all in balance and ready for food such as a mild coconut-curried shrimp; or, popcorn if you're keepin' it simple!

Kitchen Survivor™ Grade: B

Your notes: _____

Chateau Ste. Michelle Canoe Ridge Estate Chardonnay, Washington 2008   **$18**   **Pts 91**

The creamy papaya, guava and coconut are the tropics in a glass. Serve it when you want to impress without breaking the bank. Great with aged Gouda.

Kitchen Survivor™ Grade: B+

Your notes: _____

Clos du Bois Sonoma Reserve Chardonnay, Russian River Valley, California 2007   **$17**   **Pts 91**

Drinks like fancy Chard, without the fancy price! Buttery, toasted marshmallow scents, vanilla and apple compote on the palate with a creamy texture and long finish. Pair with lobster or Gouda cheese.

Kitchen Survivor™ Grade: B

Your notes: _____

Chateau St. Jean Chardonnay,   **Pts**
Sonoma, California 2009   **$13**   **89**

Quality and consistency are CSJ specialties. This
Chard is balanced, with ripe pear and Fuji apple fruit
and a whiff of cinnamon-oakiness. Lovely with chow-
ders, cheesy pastas, chilled seafood and Cobb salad.
Kitchen Survivor™ Grade: B

Your notes: _____

Kali Hart Chardonnay, Monterey,   **Pts**
California 2009   **$19**   **94**

One of the lushest Chardonnays I tasted all year, and
sumptuously Monterey. That means neon tropical
fruit, papaya, pineapple, with racy tangerine and
honeysuckle. Pair with silky scallops or sweet crab.
Kitchen Survivor™ Grade: B

Your notes: _____

Kendall-Jackson Vintner's Reserve   **Pts**
Chardonnay, California 2009   **$14**   **89**

The wine that made Chardonnay America's go-to
grape. Great quality for the price thanks to unparal-
leled vineyard quality. The lush stone fruit and toasty
oak are balanced with juicy acidity. Delicious for sipping, or pairing with all things Caesar or seafood.
Kitchen Survivor™ Grade: A

Your notes: _____

Souverain Chardonnay, Alexander   **Pts**
Valley, California 2009   **$17**   **90**

Hello, honeydew! And cantaloupe, coconut and
cream. The tender texture is almost nectar-like, without being heavy. Worthy of the silkiest scallops, lobster bisque or a fine Camembert.
Kitchen Survivor™ Grade: A

Your notes: _____

Wente Riva Ranch Chardonnay,   **Pts**
Livermore, California 2009   **$17**   **90**

Buttery, tropical, honeyed, luscious - the most Chardonnay decadence for the money you can find. Pour
it when you want to impress without breaking the
bank. Serve aged Manchego cheese alongside for
extra points without a lot of fuss in the kitchen.
Kitchen Survivor™ Grade: A

Your notes: _____

Beringer Private Reserve Chardonnay, **Pts**
Napa, California 2008 $35 90

The sweet-scented nose evokes grandma's kitchen at Thanksgiving: brown sugar and baking pastry scents, and cinnamon-apple flavors with a touch of sweet vanilla. Pair with grilled shrimp or corn on the cob.
Kitchen Survivor™ Grade: B
Your notes: _____

Chappellet Chardonnay, Napa Valley, **Pts**
California 2008 $32 92

A classic Napa name that kicks many newbies' butts. Frisky fresh acidity is a great foil to the coconutty-toasty, lush tropical fruit. Pair with buttery scallops!
Kitchen Survivor™ Grade: B+
Your notes: _____

Flora Springs Barrel Fermented **Pts**
Chardonnay, Napa, California 2008 $23 90

This wine is like dessert in a glass (minus the sugar and fat - yay!) Caramelized pineapple upside-down cake fruit plus a lemon meringue pie creamy-zing. Delish with seared scallops - or popcorn & a movie!
Kitchen Survivor™ Grade: B
Your notes: _____

Franciscan Cuvee Sauvage Chardonnay, **Pts**
Napa, California 2007 $36 92

Here's Napa richness and power without excess. Layers of creamy, caramelized toffee scents frame a ripe and concentrated core of sweet apples and tropical fruits that echo into the long baking spice finish.
Kitchen Survivor™ Grade: B
Your notes: _____

Frank Family Chardonnay, **Pts**
Napa, California 2008 $33 93

This wine packs it in: a succulent spectrum of fruits from apple to honeydew to grilled pineapple, lavished with rich and sweet vanilla-cinnamon oak, all in balance. Pair with steak (yep!) and mushrooms.
Kitchen Survivor™ Grade: B
Your notes: _____

Robert Mondavi Napa Chardonnay,   **Pts**
California 2008   **$20**   **89**

Better than ever, thanks to a new depth and concentration. The baked apple, toasted pecan and honeyed notes linger into the finish. Pair with cheesy risotto.

Kitchen Survivor™ Grade: B

Your notes: _____

Rombauer Chardonnay, Carneros,   **Pts**
Napa, California 2008   **$34**   **88**

Big-Chard fans adore the super-buttery oak-lavished style that's big enough to stand up even to steak. Add sauteed mushrooms and creamy polenta-that's livin'!

Kitchen Survivor™ Grade: B+

Your notes: _____

St. Supery Oak Free Chardonnay,   **Pts**
Napa, California 2008   **$19**   **89**

Bucking the standard oaky Napa Chard formula, this stainless-fermented wine trades on exuberant and pure stone and tropical fruit and great acidity. That broadens the pairing horizons to Asian and beyond!

Kitchen Survivor™ Grade: A+

Your notes: _____

Stag's Leap Wine Cellars Karia Chardonnay,   **Pts**
Napa, California 2008   **$34**   **90**

The Cabs are Stag's Leap's calling cards so I expected subtle layers of fennel, tarragon, fresh hay and spicy potpourri to do a dance around the ripe pear fruit. Pair with seared panko-crusted tilapia. Yum!

Kitchen Survivor™ Grade: B+

Your notes: _____

Trefethen Estate Chardonnay,   **Pts**
California 2008   **$30**   **93**

Trefethen's style is unwavering: subtle, elegant, gorgeously balanced. Notes of fresh hay, sweet spice, apple compote and wet gravel grace both the nose and the finish. In the mid-palate it's all quince compote and spiced apples. At our pairing seminar it was delicious with buttered popcorn and Piave cheese.

Kitchen Survivor™ Grade: B

Your notes: _____

TOP TEN CHARDONNAYS:
NEW WORLD $20-$40

Catena Alta Chardonnay, Mendoza,   **Pts**
Argentina 2008   **$25**   **90**

Argentina's top Chard is loaded with mango and stone fruit flavors, and toasty vanilla oak scents. Pair with grilled shrimp with mango salsa, or popcorn!
Kitchen Survivor™ Grade: B
Your notes: _____

Chalk Hill Estate Chardonnay, Chalk Hill,   **Pts**
Russian River Valley, California 2008   **$35**   **97**

A triumph of finesse and opulence, with subtle toasty minerality and caramelized notes, overlaying a core of sumptuous stone fruit and deft toffee-toasty oakiness. This is America's Chassagne-Montrachet, and it can age like one. Pair with buttery lobster or truffle risotto.
Kitchen Survivor™ Grade: B+
Your notes: _____

Chateau Ste. Michelle Cold Creek   **Pts**
Chardonnay, Washington 2008   **$22**   **90**

This wine is all buttercream in the nose and spicy cinnamon apples on the creamy palate, without being heavy. Pair with a silky fish like snapper or halibut.
Kitchen Survivor™ Grade: A+
Your notes: _____

Chateau St. Jean Robert Young Chardonnay,   **Pts**
Alexander Valley, California 2007   **$25**   **92**

A CA classic with a Burgundy-like nuttiness, vivid honeyed pear flavors, soft cinnamon spice and great length. Bring out the minerals with trout amandine.
Kitchen Survivor™ Grade: B+
Your notes: _____

Matanzas Creek Chardonnay, Sonoma   **Pts**
Valley, California 2008   **$29**   **92**

A classic whose Meursault-like toasty minerality and rich baked apple fruit make it a great partner for mushroom dishes and aged cheeses.
Kitchen Survivor™ Grade: B
Your notes: _____

Mer Soleil 'Silver' Unoaked Chardonnay,   **Pts**
Santa Lucia Highlands, California 2008   **$26**   **94**

One of my Delta picks, whose exotic tropical fruit will feel like a trip to Hawaii or at least, Trader Vic's! "Silver" refers to the stainless fermentation tanks that let the mango-guava fruit shine through for yummy sipping, and for pairing with Asian and spicy fare.

Kitchen Survivor™ Grade: B+

Your notes: _____

Rodney Strong Reserve Chardonnay,   **Pts**
Russian River Valley, California 2007   **$40**   **91**

Tasted blind, we guessed this was twice the price! It is creamy, juicy butterscotch decadence in a glass. Pair with scallops in browned butter sauce.

Kitchen Survivor™ Grade: B

Your notes: _____

Sonoma-Cutrer Russian River Ranches   **Pts**
Chardonnay, California 2009   **$21**   **91**

The perfect pedigree for a Delta pick! Plus, the lovely fruit intensity - vivid stone fruits and pineapple framed by soft vanilla oakiness - is sure to please at 30,000 feet, on its own and with food whether salty, seafood-y, smoky or spicy. It's also great with cheese.

Kitchen Survivor™ Grade: B+

Your notes: _____

Sbragia Family Home Ranch Chardonnay,   **Pts**
Dry Creek Valley, California 2008   **$26**   **92**

This wine delivers super-opulence for a great price. It's loaded with golden pineapple, mango and marzipan notes, plus an unctuous texture that'll make you swoon. Pair with lobster, mushrooms or duck confit.

Kitchen Survivor™ Grade: B+

Your notes: _____

Talbott (Robert) Sleepy Hollow Chardonnay,   **Pts**
Santa Lucia Highlands, California 2008   **$38**   **95**

Consistent, original, irresistible. You can count on the lush mango, singed banana and passion fruit style every vintage. The great acidity that makes it a lovely match with buttery lobster or hoisin-barbecued salmon is always there, too.

Kitchen Survivor™ Grade: A

Your notes: _____

Antinori Cervaro della Sala Chardonnay/   **Pts**
Grechetto, Umbria, Italy 2008   **$50**   **95**

As good as great Burgundy, with its minerality, purity of crisp apple and lemon fruit, stony nutty toastiness, and superb balance. Pair with scallops.

Kitchen Survivor™ Grade: B

Your notes: _____

Far Niente Estate Chardonnay,   **Pts**
California 2008   **$56**   **90**

California fruit, French-style subtlety, with a spicy-nutty-stony minerality, gentle vanilla oak and a dense core of ripe pineapple. It can age, but pairs well now with seared halibut on a bed of caramelized leeks.

Kitchen Survivor™ Grade: A+

Your notes: _____

Grgich Hills Estate Chardonnay, Napa,   **Pts**
California 2008   **$42**   **94**

Another "wow" Grgich with layers a-go-go: intense Asian pear and Fuji apple fruit, wet stone and rose-hips minerality and soft oak, all on a taut wire of acidity that makes it great for cellaring, and tasty to pair now with seafood, polenta, and mushroom dishes.

Kitchen Survivor™ Grade: A

Your notes: _____

Kistler Vine Hill Vineyard Chardonnay,   **Pts**
Russian River Valley, California 2007   **$125**   **94**

An icon, known for its balance between succulent stone fruit, minerals, and nutty browned butter and mushroom notes - a love letter to truffle dishes!

Kitchen Survivor™ Grade: B+

Your notes: _____

Leeuwin Estate Art Series Chardonnay,   **Pts**
Margaret River, Australia 2006   **$89**   **94**

Old world scents of beeswax, honey, chamomile and white blossoms; new world fruit intensity with flavors of lemon curd and pineapple; long finish of toast, cream and honey; excellent ageability. Seek it out.

Kitchen Survivor™ Grade: B+

Your notes: _____

Newton Unfiltered Chardonnay,   **Pts**
Napa, California 2007   **$48**   **92**

A Napa classic, with marzipan and caramelized pear notes, toastiness and an alluring satiny texture. The best match: miso-glazed black cod a la Nobu NYC.

Kitchen Survivor™ Grade: B+

Your notes: _____

Ramey Wine Cellars Hyde Vyd Chardonnay   **Pts**
Carneros, Napa, California 2007   **$60**   **96**

California's Montrachet? The lush ripe apple and tropical fruit, luxuriant texture and vivid acidity and minerality say yes. With age it gets nutty-truffly. I paired it with lobster with vanilla bean butter. OMG.

Kitchen Survivor™ Grade: B+

Your notes: _____

Ridge Vineyard Santa Cruz Mountains   **Pts**
Estate Chardonnay, Santa Cruz, CA 2008   **$40**   **97**

Meet California's Corton-Charlemagne: detailed and complex, with a toasty stony scent, deep baked apple, cinnamon and quince paste notes, an expansive mid-palate, and a long, spicy finish. Pair with truffle pasta.

Kitchen Survivor™ Grade: B+

Your notes: _____

Shafer Red Shoulder Ranch,   **Pts**
Chardonnay, Carneros, California 2008   **$48**   **95**

Toffee and golden pineapple scents, with deep apple compote, allspice and toasted brioche on the palate and finish. A wow match with seared scallops.

Kitchen Survivor™ Grade: A

Your notes: _____

Staglin Family Estate Chardonnay,   **Pts**
Napa, California 2008   **$75**   **96**

One of the best California Chardonnays, period, and also one of the most Burgundian, with a Puligny-like talcum and wet gravel minerality, white flowers and creme brulee scent, and a tight core of concentrated cinnamon-apple fruit. Will age 10 years, easy.

Kitchen Survivor™ Grade: A+

Your notes: _____

TOP TEN CHARDONNAYS: FRENCH WHITE BURGUNDY

Cave de Lugny Macon-Lugny 'Les Charmes', Burgundy, France 2008   **$11**   Pts 89

Why pay more? This elegant chamomile-tea-and-apples Burgundy and a plate of oysters or an herbed omelet is an instant escape to Paris, for cheap!
Kitchen Survivor™ Grade: A
Your notes: _____

Chartron & Trebuchet Rully La Chaume, Burgundy, France 2008   **$18**   Pts 89

The kumquat-citrus flavor and rosehips minerality of this wine are softened by a juicy-apple palate that keeps you sipping. Pair with shallot-steamed mussels.
Kitchen Survivor™ Grade: A
Your notes: _____

Joseph Drouhin Pouilly-Fuisse (*poo-YEE fwee-SAY*), France 2008   **$30**   Pts 89

Fresh almonds, crisp apples and a hint of citrus, plus a creamy roundness and long finish that sets this P-F apart from the pack. Pair with caper-butter trout.
Kitchen Survivor™ Grade: A
Your notes: _____

Domaine Laroche Chablis St. Martin, Burgundy, France 2008   **$30**   Pts 89

Honeysuckle and Fuji apple notes leap from the glass and dance softly on the palate and finish. The crisp acidity and makes this wine great for fried chicken.
Kitchen Survivor™ Grade: A
Your notes: _____

Domaine Leflaive Puligny-Montrachet, Burgundy, France 2008   **$100**   Pts 92

A benchmark white Burgundy, pricey because there is so little made. The wine always shows notes of wet stones, lemon, chamomile and white flowers, touched with just a whiff of exotic coconut and honey. Great with seared scallops in brown butter sauce or for total decadence, truffled risotto.
Kitchen Survivor™ Grade: A
Your notes: _____

Domaine Vincent Girardin Pouilly-Fuisse   **Pts**
Vieilles Vignes, Burgundy, France 2009   **$28**   **90**

Vieilles Vignes or "old vines," yield lots of complexity: lovely wet stone minerality, and scents of apple peel and white blossoms. I chose this for Delta because the extra intensity, and the lively acidity, will show beautifully even at 30,000 feet, solo or with food.

Kitchen Survivor™ Grade: A

Your notes: _____

M. Colin Saint-Aubin En Remilly,   **Pts**
Burgundy, France 2008   **$35**   **93**

Although not cheap, this competes in complexity with Burgundies 2-3X the price. The bewitching layers of vanilla, toasted hazelnuts, grilled pineapple and mushrooms are a window into why white Burgundy is so famous. Pair with mushroom or truffle risotto.

Kitchen Survivor™ Grade: A

Your notes: _____

Louis Jadot Pouilly-Fuisse,   **Pts**
Burgundy, France 2008   **$24**   **89**

Fresh scents of hay, lemon zest, talcum powder and green apple are the signatures of this classic. It's a lovely match for sushi, or a creamy Camembert.

Kitchen Survivor™ Grade: A

Your notes: _____

Louis Latour Corton-Charlemagne,   **Pts**
Burgundy, France 2008   **$95**   **95**

Corton "Charlie" is the model for all great barrel-aged Chards. The rich scent of baking fruit tarts and deep core of apple-quince compote echo in the palate and long, spicy finish. A great ager, and a superb match for roast quail with root vegetables and mushrooms.

Kitchen Survivor™ Grade: A

Your notes: _____

Olivier Leflaive Meursault,   **Pts**
Burgundy, France 2008   **$40**   **91**

A top entry-level Meursault, with the classic character of wet stones and toasted hazelnuts, dried apples and a touch of cinnamon, and a good grip of acidity. My favorite match is mushroom ravioli.

Kitchen Survivor™ Grade: A

Your notes: _____

Uncommon White Grapes & Blends

Category Profile: Welcome to one of the coolest sections of the book! A label of "Uncommon" for wines that don't fit neatly into a major category means some may not get the respect they deserve. But trust me, here is where you will find the gems in terms of deliciousness and uniqueness for the price. The group comprises a diverse collection of wine types, including uncommon regions, grapes, or blends. Here is some background on each:

Uncommon Grapes and Regions—This category includes the grapes Albarino (from Spain), Pinot Blanc, Gewurztraminer, Gruner-Veltliner (from Austria; beloved by sommeliers and called by its pet name, Gru-V, like groovy), Torrontes (from Argentina), Chenin Blanc (indigenous to France's Loire Valley and widespread in South Africa under the synonym Steen) and Viognier (indigenous to France's Rhone Valley), all definitely worth your attention. The other-than-Pinot-Grigio Italian whites are also here, along with Spanish regional whites. (See the "Wine List Decoder" for more on these.)

Unique Blends—France's Alsace wineries sometimes blend the local grapes of the region - Riesling, Gewurztraminer, Pinot Gris and Pinot Blanc among others. This category also includes other specialty multi-grape blends from all over the globe that are well worth trying. Maybe it's a sign that consumers are continuing to branch out. Yay!

Serve: Well chilled.

When: The uncommon grapes (like Gewurztraminer) and unique blends are wonderful when you want to surprise guests with a different flavor experience.

With: In my opinion, Gewurztraminer, Albarino, Gruner-Veltliner, Torrontes and the unusual grape blends are some of the most fun food partners out there. They are especially suited to spicy ethnic fare such as Chinese, Thai and Indian. Also them with barbecue and even the Thanksgiving feast!

In: The One™ glass for white, or an all-purpose wineglass.

Almost Top 10 Uncommon Whites:

These wines are also well worth checking out:
Hugel Gewurztraminer
Pierre Sparr Alsace One
Hirsch Gruner-Veltliner #1
Hogue Gewurztraminer
Anselmi Soave
Teruzzi & Puthod Vernaccia
Umani Ronchi Verdicchio
Sigalas Assyrtiko
Boutari Moscofilero
Miner Viognier

Emerging & "worth the splurge":

Calera Mt. Harlan Viognier
Bastianich Vespa
Jermann Vintage Tunina
Weinbach Muscat
Naia Albarino
Godeval Godello
Remirez de Ganuza Rioja Blanco

Albert Boxler Muscat Grand Cru Brand,   **Pts**
Alsace, France 2008   **$40**   **97**

A majestic wine layered with honeysuckle, apricot, pink grapefruit, quince, fig, plus sweet spices on the long finish. A classic match is Muenster cheese but I'd go aged Gouda. Great on the Thanksgiving table.
Kitchen Survivor™ Grade: B
Your notes: _____

Brundlmayer Gruner Veltliner Kamptaler   **Pts**
Terrassen, Austria 2009   **$19**   **94**

Tingly-savory white pepper, sage and cucumber in the scent, zippy grapefruit, vitamin C and apple on the palate. Great with pork with Dijon mustard sauce.
Kitchen Survivor™ Grade: B+
Your notes: _____

Heidi Schrock Ried Vogelsang blend,   **Pts**
Neusiedlersee-Hugelland, Austria 2009   **$16**   **90**

The grapes - Welschriesling, Pinot Blanc, gold Muscat and Furmint - are a frisky mouthful, and so is the wine. It's floral and tutti-frutti aromatherapy for your senses, and a love letter to Chinese, Thai or sushi.
Kitchen Survivor™ Grade: B
Your notes: _____

Fred Loimer 'Lois' Gruner Veltliner,   **Pts**
Austria 2009   **$12**   **89**

A great starter GruV, with pink grapefruit, white pepper and ginger from nose to finish. Break out the horseradishy cocktail sauce and chilled shrimp.
Kitchen Survivor™ Grade: B
Your notes: _____

Hugel Pinot Blanc Cuvee Les Amours,   **Pts**
Alsace, France 2009   **$15**   **91**

In a blind tasting with pricier Alsace whites, this blew me away. The creamy-mushroomy-stony layers, juicy apple-pear flavor and length were *amazing*. A great foil for fried foods, strong cheeses, briny shellfish.
Kitchen Survivor™ Grade: B
Your notes: _____

Laurenz "Singing" Gruner-Veltliner,   **Pts**
Austria 2009   **$15**   **90**

Amazingly seductive, with marzipan, quince paste
and pear frangipane flavors, all with great acidity,
frisky minerality and a long finish. Pair with BBQ.
Kitchen Survivor™ Grade: B

Your notes: _____

Nigl Gruner-Veltliner Alte Reben,   **Pts**
Kremstal, Austria 2009   **$30**   **94**

Creamy marzipan and Asian pear are this wine's signatures, along with fragrant fig, tarragon and a touch
of grapefruit that linger into the long, savory finish.
Try it with frisee, walnut and blue cheese salad.
Kitchen Survivor™ Grade: B

Your notes: _____

Pierre Sparr Pinot Blanc Reserve,   **Pts**
Alsace, France 2008   **$14**   **90**

This value is one of the top Alsace wines I've had all
year! The lip-smacking pineapple and kumquat fruit
pairs great with spicy sushi, blackened fish or BBQ.
Kitchen Survivor™ Grade: B

Your notes: _____

Schloss Gobelsburg Gruner-Veltliner   **Pts**
Gobelsburger, Kamptal, Austria 2009   **$14**   **92**

This super-value offering from a great producer is
bright with grapefruit, Chinese mustard and green
apple notes. Pairing with savory (not sweet) barbecue
or leeks with vinaigrette plays up the wine's spice.
Kitchen Survivor™ Grade: A

Your notes: _____

Setzer Gruner Veltliner Ausstich,   **Pts**
Weinviertel, Austria 2009   **$16**   **92**

The chalkiness and laser-pure grapefruit notes don't
prepare you for the tender pear flavor and creamy texture. This wine with age is an amazing surprise. At
this price get some for now with fried foods, salads
and charcuterie, and some to hold. At 10 years, it
gains a creme brulee-like richness. Yum!
Kitchen Survivor™ Grade: A+

Your notes: _____

TOP TEN UNCOMMON WHITES: NEW WORLD

Crios Torrontes, Cafayate, Mendoza, Argentina 2009   **$14**   **Pts 90**

A bottle of perfume and a bouquet of flowers on Valentine's Day or, how about this fragrant little number that you can afford (and share) a lot more often? The seductive jasmine, honeysuckle and tutti frutti scents and flavors are every bit as romantic, too. Pick up some Tex Mex, barbecue, sushi or Chinese and add a little spice to your takeout night!

Kitchen Survivor™ Grade: A+

Your notes: _____

Dry Creek Vineyard Dry Chenin Blanc, Clarksburg, California 2009   **$11**   **Pts 88**

Like biting a Golden Delicious apple—juicy, with snappy acidity and a creamy-waxy finish. De-lish on its own and with cheeses, salads and spicy dishes.

Kitchen Survivor™ Grade: B

Your notes: _____

Fetzer Valley Oaks Gewurztraminer, California 2008   **$7**   **Pts 87**

Great Gewurz character of ginger, apricot, lychee and rose petals on the nose. The soft apricot sweetness sparked with acidity make it great with spicy curries.

Kitchen Survivor™ Grade: B

Your notes: _____

Gougenheim Torrontes, Mendoza, Argentina 2009   **$12**   **Pts 90**

A Delta pick because the juicy tropical and floral notes of this wine will soar even at 30,000 feet. Great with shellfish, and Indian, Moroccan and Asian fare.

Kitchen Survivor™ Grade: A

Your notes: _____

Kanu Chenin Blanc, Stellenbosch, South Africa 2009   **$9**   **Pts 89**

Like a bowl of crisp golden delicious apples with fresh cream. This light and sprightly, super-value, no oak wine is delicious and goes with anything!

Kitchen Survivor™ Grade: A

Your notes: _____

Miner Family Viognier Simpson Vineyard,
California 2008 $20 Pts 94

A top CA Viognier for its varietal character - tangerine, honeysuckle, mango and lavender without heaviness. Pair with seared scallops with citrus cream.
Kitchen Survivor™ Grade: A

Your notes: _____

Qupe Marsanne, Santa Ynez, Valley,
California 2009 $18 Pts 94

Fragrant lily, peach, apricot and honeysuckle notes make this a blast to pair with fusion flavors, whether Latin, Asian, BBQ or Tex Mex. One sip and you're hooked!
Kitchen Survivor™ Grade: B

Your notes: _____

Sokol Blosser Evolution,
Oregon NV $15 Pts 89

Like an aromatherapy treatment—honeysuckle, hyacinth, peach, apricot, kumquat—but a lot cheaper! It's yummy with summer veggies and anything barbecued, from shrimp to ribs. Great with sushi, too.
Kitchen Survivor™ Grade: B

Your notes: _____

Tablas Creek Cotes de Tablas Blanc,
Paso Robles, California 2008 $22 Pts 91

French-style aromatic complexity - fennel, flowers, quince and pears, with California ripeness. It's a blend of Viognier, Roussanne, Marsanne and Grenache Blanc that's great with ceviche and Tex Mex but loves sophisticated fare like duck or pate, too.
Kitchen Survivor™ Grade: A

Your notes: _____

Zaca Mesa Viognier, Santa Ynez Valley,
California 2008 $19 Pts 91

Hello, gorgeous! Look up tropical fruit in the dictionary and I bet you see this label. The wine drips with mango, banana, guava and white peach flavors, all balanced by lovely acidity. The jasmine-peach fragrance is as wearable as perfume. Pair with creamy butternut squash bisque or sweet seared scallops.
Kitchen Survivor™ Grade: A

Your notes: _____

TOP TEN UNCOMMON WHITES: OLD WORLD

Bastianich Friulano, Friuli   **Pts**
Italy 2008   **$18**   **90**

This wine from famed restaurateur Joe Bastianich is all fresh almond, floral, ripe pear freshness. A choice chaser for prosciutto, and great with mussels.
Kitchen Survivor™ Grade: B+
Your notes: _____

Guado al Tasso Vermentino, Bolgheri,   **Pts**
Tuscany, Italy 2009   **$22**   **91**

From scent to finish, a real "wow" wine. Intense aromatics of ripest peach, lemon oil and tropical blossoms are followed by pure Asian pear flavors and a long, almond brioche finish. Pair with smoked pork.
Kitchen Survivor™ Grade: A+
Your notes: _____

Inama "Vin Soave," Soave Classico,   **Pts**
Veneto, Italy 2008   **$17**   **90**

Not your grandmother's Soave. This one is fantastic, with scents of Seckel pear, fennel, almonds and talcum powder that echo on the palate and into the long finish. Great with fried foods, and even artichokes!
Kitchen Survivor™ Grade: B
Your notes: _____

Hidalgo La Gitana (*ee-DAHL-go   **Pts**
***la hee-TAH-nuh*) Manzanilla**   **$16**   **90**
Sherry, Spain NV

Drink Sherry, baby! The real thing (from Spain). With food. This utterly unique sherry has a bracing tang along with notes of olive oil and herbs and an almond finish. Serve it with salty-gamy Serrano ham.
Kitchen Survivor™ Grade: A
Your notes: _____

Lopez de Heredia Rioja Blanco Crianza,   **Pts**
Rioja, Spain 2000   **$25**   **92**

A like-no-other wine with bottle-aged notes of consomme, beeswax, butter, honey, chamomile and nuts. Pair with aged cheeses or a subtle mushroom pasta.
Kitchen Survivor™ Grade: C
Your notes: _____

Marques de Riscal Rueda (*mar-KESS*   **Pts**
***deh ree-SCAHL roo-AY-duh*), Spain 2009**   **$9**   **89**

This wine put Rueda (the region name) on the map, and now this white made from the local Verdejo grape is on fire. Riscal's key lime and kiwi fruit, without oak flavor, makes it a great food partner: salads, ceviche, goat cheese, garlicky pastas and Spanish chorizo. *Kitchen Survivor™ Grade: B*

Your notes: _____

Martin Codax Albarino, Rias Baixas   **Pts**
(*all-buh-REEN-yo*), Spain 2009   **$15**   **89**

Textbook Albarino, with snappy green apple fruit and notes of fresh hay, chalk and candied lemon. A natural with fresh shellfish, and great with goat cheese. *Kitchen Survivor™ Grade: B*

Your notes: _____

Palacios Remondo Placet Rioja Blanco,   **Pts**
Rioja, Spain 2007   **$23**   **89**

At once exotically fragrant with tropical blossoms, and snappy with minerality and crisp citrus-pear notes. Delicious just for sipping but also a fab food partner with hard cheeses, shellfish and spicy fare. *Kitchen Survivor™ Grade: B*

Your notes: _____

Sella & Mosca La Cala Vermentino,   **Pts**
Sardinia, Italy 2009   **$13**   **89**

Echoes of the pineapple Lifesavers of my childhood, without the sugar! There's also lovely acidity and a lively rosehips minerality that makes this a great partner for cured meats, olive tapenade or clam pasta. *Kitchen Survivor™ Grade: A*

Your notes: _____

Villa Sparina Gavi di Gavi,   **Pts**
Piedmont, Italy 2009   **$17**   **90**

The fresh apple, hay, chamomile and buttermilk notes in this wine leap out of the glass and say "drink me" with almost anything - salads, sandwiches, light pastas, cured meats, even brunch fare. Easy, yummy! *Kitchen Survivor™ Grade: A*

Your notes: _____

ROSÉ WINES

Category Profile: Although many buyers are snobby about the blush category, the truth is that for most of us white Zinfandel was probably the first wine we drank that had a cork. It's a juicy, uncomplicated style that makes a lot of buyers, and their wallets, very happy. In every previous edition of the guide I included White Zin and other sweet-ish blush wines. This year I decided that folks don't really need me to weigh in on blush wine. People choose according to price and brand familiarity and for good reason: they are all decent sipping wines and all very similar in taste. They offer uncomplicated, inexpensive, festive refreshment and everyone "gets it." No Master Sommelier needed.

Now for the gear switch—rosé. The only thing true rosés have in common with the blush category is appearance. Rosé wines are classic to many world-class European wine regions. They are absolutely dry, tangy, crisp, and amazingly interesting wines for the money. I often say that with their spice and complexity they have red wine flavor, but the lightness of body and chillability gives them white wine style. They are *great* food wines. Don't miss the chance to try my recommendations or those of your favorite shop or restaurant. You will love them.

Serve: The colder the better.

When: Rosés are great for both sipping and meals. Their layers of flavor and excellent acidity make them some of the most food-versatile wines in the world.

With: A touch of sweetness in wine can tone down heat, so spicy foods are an especially good partner for blush wine. Dry rosés go with everything.

In: The One™ glass for white, or an all-purpose wineglass.

Almost Top Ten Rosés

There are so many great rosés for great prices that come summer, you should try every single one you can get your hands on. Ask at the shop or just take a gamble on the cheap ones because I've never had a bad dry rosé. The below wines are all worth checking out, too:

Robert Sinskey Pinot Noir Rosé
Domaine Ott Bandol Rosé
Regaleali Rosato
Chivite Navarra Rosado
Marques de Caceres Rioja Rosado
Vega Sindoa Rosado
Balland Sancerre Rosé
Chapoutier Cotes du Rhone Rosé
Borsao Rosado

TOP TEN ROSÉS

Bodegas Muga Rioja Rosado,
Spain 2009 $12   **Pts** 89

Red and white grapes are blended to make this straw-
berry-pomegranate "gulper" that's delish with spicy
foods like the Spanish classic sausage, chorizo.
Kitchen Survivor™ Grade: B

Your notes: _____

Bodegas Ochoa (oh-*CHOH*-uh)
Garnacha Rosado, Spain 2009 $9   **Pts** 88

A wonderful summer rosé, completely dry yet juicy
with strawberry-rhubarb flavors kicked up with a
touch of white pepper. Great with BBQ shrimp.
Kitchen Survivor™ Grade: B+

Your notes: _____

Bonny Doon Vin Gris de Cigare
Pink Wine, California 2009 $12   **Pts** 89

This wine boldly intro'd the European dry rosé style at
the height of blush-wine mania. The juicy-spicy notes
and blood orange fruit are perfect for summer grilling.
Kitchen Survivor™ Grade: B

Your notes: _____

Chateau d'Aqueria Tavel Rosé,
Provence, France 2009 $19   **Pts** 90

Summer's bounty in a bottle: strawberries, sweet tomatoes and watermelon, plus a savory herb note that
makes it a match for anything Mediterranean or grilled.
Kitchen Survivor™ Grade: B+

Your notes: _____

Chateau d'Eclans Whispering Angel
Rosé, Cotes de Provence, France 2009 $18   **Pts** 89

Pale onion-skin color, racy pomegranate, pink grapefruit and spice notes - that's classic Provence rosé, perfect for olive tapenade, spicy sausage and goat cheese.
Kitchen Survivor™ Grade: B+

Your notes: _____

Domaine Tempier Bandol Rosé,   **Pts**
Provence, France 2008   **$25**   **92**

Expensive for rosé, but this is the famous Provencal classic: faded onion-skin color, pomegranate fruit, white pepper and savory herb notes, plus lots of refreshing acidity. It's tailor-made for Nicoise salad.
Kitchen Survivor™ Grade: B

Your notes: _____

El Coto Rioja Rosado,   **Pts**
Spain 2009   **$11**   **91**

Always one of my favorite rosés, for its depth of strawberry flavor, snappy acidity and wonderful white pepper spice that match piquillo peppers, chorizo and other Spanish tapas perfectly.
Kitchen Survivor™ Grade: A

Your notes: _____

Etude Pinot Noir Rosé,   **Pts**
Carneros, California 2009   **$16**   **91**

The sweet strawberry and pie cherry notes and a touch of spiciness are pumped-up by vibrant acidity that keeps you sippin' and matchin' - try this with goat cheese crostini sprinkled with pomegranate seeds, or a smoked ham and gruyere omelet.
Kitchen Survivor™ Grade: A

Your notes: _____

Lopez de Heredia Tondonia Rosado   **Pts**
Gran Reserva, Rioja, Spain 2000   **$26**   **93**

Like all Lopez de Heredia wines, a like-no-other Rioja due to the extensive bottle age which creates amazing complexity. Mushroom consomme, cured meat, potpourri, balsamic and herb-infused olive oil scents and flavors make it a foodie's dream wine, but mushrooms and Serrano ham are the perfect pairings.
Kitchen Survivor™ Grade: C

Your notes: _____

Miner Family Sangiovese Rosato Gibson   **Pts**
Ranch, Mendocino, California 2008   **$16**   **92**

One whiff of the cran-raspberry, orange peel and potpourri perfume of this wine gets your mouth watering, for a sip and a plate of something savory and summery - like BBQ'd shrimp - to go alongside.
Kitchen Survivor™ Grade: B

Your notes: _____

RED WINES

Pinot Noir

Category Profile: Pinot Noir is my favorite of the major classic red grape varieties, because I love its smoky-earthiness; pure fruit flavor; and, most of all, silken texture. When well made, it offers red wine intensity and complexity, without being heavy. Although Pinot Noir's home turf is the Burgundy region of France, few of those wines make the list of top sellers in the United States, because production is tiny. (As such, my Top Ten list focuses largely on "entry-level" wines that are relatively available and affordable.) The coolest parts of coastal California (especially the Russian River Valley, Carneros, Monterey, Sonoma Coast, and Santa Barbara County) specialize in Pinot Noir, as does Oregon's Willamette (*will-AM-ett*) Valley. New Zealand is also growing in importance as a Pinot source, making some of the best in my Top Ten value category. Pinot Noir from all the major regions is typically oak aged, but as with other grapes the amount of oakiness is matched to the intensity of the fruit. Generally the budget bottlings have the least amount of oak aging.

Serve: *Cool* room temperature; don't hesitate to chill the bottle briefly if needed.

When: Although the silky texture makes Pinot Noir quite bewitching on its own, it is also the ultimate "food wine." It is my choice to take to dinner parties and to order in restaurants, because I know it will probably delight both white and red wine drinkers and will go with most any food.

With: Pinot's versatility is legendary, but it is *the* wine for mushroom dishes, salmon, rare tuna, and any bird (especially duck). Smoked meats and fish, too.

In: The One™ glass for red wines, or a larger-bowled red wineglass.

Almost Top Ten Pinots:

These wines are also well worth checking out:
Saintsbury
Sanford
Gary Farrell
Davis Bynum
Schug
Joseph Swan
Kent Rasmussen
Domaine Carneros
David Bruce
Deloach
Robert Sinskey
Acacia
Chalone

Emerging & "worth the splurge":

Furthermore Wines
DuMol
Belle Glos
Sea Smoke
Cobb Wines
Three Sticks

TOP TEN PINOT NOIRS:
NEW WORLD UNDER $20

Au Bon Climat Santa Maria Valley Pinot   **Pts**
Noir, Santa Barbara, California 2008   **$18**   **93**
Oh-bohn-clee-MAHT - the many fans call it "ABC" -
is one of the top US Pinots, packing layers of rasp-
berry fruit, black tea, a gamy earthiness, and perfect
balance - all for an amazing price. Also check out
ABC's many single vineyards, and cellar them. Pair
with bacon-y lentils or roasted beets with goat cheese.
Kitchen Survivor™ Grade: B+
Your notes: _____

Brancott Vineyards South Island   **Pts**
Pinot Noir, New Zealand 2009   **$14**   **89**
I like this better than the Reserve, and the value price
for such great varietal character is a gift. The sour
cherry and smoked tomato notes are a great match for
savory-sweet BBQ sauces and grilled sausages.
Kitchen Survivor™ Grade: B
Your notes: _____

Carmel Road Pinot Noir,   **Pts**
Monterey, California 2008   **$17**   **89**
This wine is all smoke, tangy raspberries and rhubarb
on the nose and palate, and soft earth in the finish.
Fabulous paired with a smoked mozzarella panini.
Kitchen Survivor™ Grade: B

Your notes: _____

Castle Rock Pinot Noir, Mendocino   **Pts**
California 2009   **$14**   **90**
Succulent, pretty and pure, with cherry pie filling and
spice notes. The satiny texture begs for salmon sushi.
Kitchen Survivor™ Grade: C
Your notes: _____

Chateau St. Jean Sonoma Pinot Noir,   **Pts**
California 2008   **$19**   **90**
An exotic riff on Pinot, with black raspberry and Chi-
nese five-spice notes. Highlight the succulent texture
by pairing with rare salmon or duck breast.
Kitchen Survivor™ Grade: B+
Your notes: _____

Kendall-Jackson Vintner's Reserve   **Pts**
Pinot Noir, California 2009   **$18**   **89**

This is a superb intro to Pinot, with spicy-silky cherry and strawberry compote flavors and a hint of vanilla. Its lively acidity and delicacy are great with mild cheeses such as Gouda, Brebis or Saint-Nectaire.
Kitchen Survivor™ Grade: B
Your notes: _____

Mark West Pinot Noir,   **Pts**
California 2009   **$15**   **89**

Tangy, silky and creamy like strawberry yogurt with a touch of spice on the palate - tailor-made for tandoori chicken or a chicken salad with dried cranberries.
Kitchen Survivor™ Grade: B
Your notes: _____

Robert Mondavi Private Selection   **Pts**
Pinot Noir, California 2008   **$11**   **87**

The 2008 sustains this wine's track record as a value star. A hint of smoke and orange peel in the scent and a light-as-a-feather strawberry-rhubarb palate make this a great partner for delicate dishes such as herb-sauteed sole or trout, or avocado and crab salad.
Kitchen Survivor™ Grade: B
Your notes: _____

Rosemount Diamond Label Pinot Noir,   **Pts**
South Eastern Australia 2009   **$11**   **87**

Quite a bit of complexity for the money, with sweet balsamic and cured meat notes along with pomegranate flavors. A nice match for pates and soft cheeses.
Kitchen Survivor™ Grade: C
Your notes: _____

Ritual by Veramonte Pinot Noir,   **Pts**
Casablanca Valley, Chile 2008   **$18**   **90**

Truly exciting Chilean Pinot Noir - this is unprecedented. Here's to the Huneeus family's commitment to genuine character - in this case gamy/animal notes, dark berries and smoke, rhubarb, and a lovely satin texture. Pair with duck or hot-smoked salmon.
Kitchen Survivor™ Grade: C
Your notes: _____

TOP TEN PINOT NOIRS: CALIFORNIA $20-$40

Calera Central Coast Pinot Noir, California 2008 $24   Pts 93

More exciting than many pricier Pinots, with silky-smoky raspberries and gamy notes on the palate, plus a satiny succulence and soft earthiness that pairs great with tender mushrooms or pillow-soft gnocchi. *Kitchen Survivor™ Grade: B+*

Your notes: _____

Cambria (*CAME-bree-uh*) Julia's Vineyard Pinot Noir, California 2008 $22   Pts 90

I love this wine's pumped-up cherry kirsch scents and flavors, kissed with notes of sweet baking spices. Play on the exotic notes by pairing with five-spice duck, Moroccan couscous, or pork with a spicy fig stuffing. *Kitchen Survivor™ Grade: B*

Your notes: _____

Deloach Russian River Pinot Noir, California 2008 $24   Pts 89

This wine offers earthy-smoky, cinnamon-spiced rhu-barb jam flavors and a snappy acidity that pairs well with pates, mild sausages and roast turkey. *Kitchen Survivor™ Grade: B*

Your notes: _____

Dutton-Goldfield Dutton Ranch Pinot Noir, Russian River Valley, California 2008 $38   Pts 92

Sweet strawberry fruit wrapped in a cloak of smoke, pipe tobacco and autumn leaf notes. Play up the earthiness by pairing with roasted root vegetables, mushroom ravioli, or pork chops with bacon-y lentils. *Kitchen Survivor™ Grade: A*

Your notes: _____

Etude Carneros Pinot Noir, California 2008 $40   Pts 96

So pretty and elegant, with sweet red currant and strawberry jam notes as well as savory coriander, car-damom, fennel seed, smoke and a long mineral-tarra-gon finish. Pair with a subtle cheese or rare tuna. *Kitchen Survivor™ Grade: A*

Your notes: _____

La Crema Sonoma Russian River   **Pts**
Valley Pinot Noir, California 2008   **$22**   **92**

Smoky spice, red currant and raspberry fruit, a long finish, and mouthwatering acidity that's just waiting for a dining partner. Great with a simple smoked or slow-cooked pork dish, or a Manchego cheese panini.
Kitchen Survivor™ Grade: A+

Your notes: _____

MacMurray Ranch Central Coast   **Pts**
Pinot Noir, California 2008   **$20**   **90**

Cedary-spicy and cranberry flavors, a mushroomy-truffly finish, and elegant texture, all at a price that loves you back. Pair with a cheese-y herbed pasta.
Kitchen Survivor™ Grade: B

Your notes: _____

Meiomi by Belle Glos Pinot Noir,   **Pts**
Sonoma Coast, California 2008   **$25**   **93**

A Delta pick, whose bewitching scents of sweet balsamic, dark cherries, hoisin sauce and baking spices are a sensory treat even at 30,000 feet! Pair with pork tenderloin, or pasta with butter and sage.
Kitchen Survivor™ Grade: B

Your notes: _____

Robert Mondavi Pinot Noir,   **Pts**
Los Carneros, California 2008   **$27**   **93**

One of my newest Delta picks and one of the top wines coming out of the Mondavi stable. I love the yin-yang of savory-sweet notes - fennel seed, black licorice, roasted plum - and the syrupy-seductive texture. A stunning match with Moroccan-spiced lamb.
Kitchen Survivor™ Grade: B

Your notes: _____

Lynmar Pinot Noir, Russian River Valley,   **Pts**
California 2008   **$40**   **92**

I love this wine's gamy, heady rhubarb, strawberry and sweet pipe tobacco flavors and its amazing satin texture and long smoky finish. Pair with silky seared tuna or roasted monkfish.
Kitchen Survivor™ Grade: B+

Your notes: _____

TOP TEN PINOT NOIRS:
CALIFORNIA OVER $40

Au Bon Climat Isabel Pinot Noir, Santa   **Pts**
Barbara, California 2007   **$47**   **96**

The lusty scents of marinating meat and berry cobbler in the oven - that is the palpable pleasure that I love in Jim Clendenen's wines. They age to complexity beyond words. Pair this with truffled roast chicken.

Kitchen Survivor™ Grade: B+

Your notes: _____

Benovia Pinot Noir, Sonoma   **Pts**
Coast, California 2008   **$42**   **91**

This wine hits on all cylinders: laser-pure cherry fruit, framed with lavish but balanced sweet oak. Everything softens and opens with air, suggesting it will age. For now, pair with pork, duck or salmon.

Kitchen Survivor™ Grade: B+

Your notes: _____

Calera Selleck Pinot Noir, Mt. Harlan,   **Pts**
California 2006   **$65**   **96**

Vintner Josh Jensen nails great Pinot, making wines with terroir that push all the pleasure buttons. This one is muscular and meaty, with beef tartare and mineral hints and sumptuous dark cherry and plum fruit.

Kitchen Survivor™ Grade: B+

Your notes: _____

Goldeneye Pinot Noir, Anderson Valley,   **Pts**
California 2007   **$55**   **92**

Anderson Valley is a rockstar PN region and this wine is Exhibit A. Cardamom, tea, rhubarb and cherry, all on a sleek and structured frame that is tasty now *and* built for aging. Fantastic with duck cassoulet.

Kitchen Survivor™ Grade: B

Your notes: _____

Merry Edwards Olivet Lane Pinot Noir,   **Pts**
Russian River Valley, California 2008   **$60**   **100**

Beg, borrow, pool funds with your wine buddies, but taste perfection, and prepare for huge pleasure payback if you cellar it. This is an uber-FAVE wine: wet slate minerality, pure, warm cherries and a coriander-tobacco savory-sweetness that unfolds, layer by layer.

Kitchen Survivor™ Grade: B

Your notes: _____

Miner Garys' Vineyard Pinot Noir, Santa   **Pts**
Lucia Highlands, California 2008   **$52** **91**
Super-ripe, red licorice-plummy and lushly oaked, but still elegant. Like cheesecake with berries (without the sugar!) when paired with Manchego cheese.
Kitchen Survivor™ Grade: B

Your notes: _____

Peay Estate Pinot Noir,   **Pts**
Sonoma Coast, California 2008   **$48** **94**
With the oak singing backup, the depth and purity of raspberry and cherry fruit with a wet slate earthiness are what get your attention. Pair with truffle risotto or silky grilled salmon with fresh thyme. Mmm!
Kitchen Survivor™ Grade: B

Your notes: _____

Pfendler Sonoma Coast Pinot Noir,   **Pts**
Sonoma Coast, California 2007   **$44** **96**
Stunningly supple and fragrant with the dark cherry, chalk and rose petal potpourri notes of a great Burgundy. Pair with roast duck or osso buco with truffle.
Kitchen Survivor™ Grade: B

Your notes: _____

Rochioli Russian River Pinot Noir,   **Pts**
California 2008   **$62** **93**
Sweet cherries and spiced herbal tea, with a gorgeous silkiness and laser purity and acidity that rings like a bell in every bottle and, carries the wine to graceful, earthy-truffly maturity for ten years easy in the cellar.
Kitchen Survivor™ Grade: B+

Your notes: _____

Williams-Selyem Pinot Noir,   **Pts**
Russian River Valley, California 2008   **$45** **96**
You have to search but it's worth it to see what Pinot as it's meant to be in America tastes like: silky-sleek, red fruits, dried flowers, delicate spices, a finish that lingers then slowly dances away. Pair it with pork, like vintner Bob Cabral does. Cellars 7-10 years, easy.
Kitchen Survivor™ Grade: B+

Your notes: _____

Brancott Reserve Pinot Noir,   **Pts**
Marlborough, New Zealand 2007   **$20**   **90**

"Delish" - how's that for a first impression? Juicy cherry pie filling flavors with a sprinkle of cinnamon, silky texture and great length. Pair with goat cheese.

Kitchen Survivor™ Grade: B

Your notes: _____

Coldstream Hills Pinot Noir, Yarra   **Pts**
Valley, Australia 2007   **$29**   **89**

I love this Aussie offering for its Burgundian subtlety. The smoky sun-dried tomato and pomegranate flavors are graced with a mushroomy earthiness that's a perfect match for sundried tomato and mushroom pasta.

Kitchen Survivor™ Grade: C

Your notes: _____

Clos Henri Pinot Noir, Marlborough,   **Pts**
New Zealand 2008   **$20**   **92**

An outstanding NZ Pinot that proves Marlborough is every bit as good for NZ PN as the vaunted Central Otago region. This one is truly Burgundian, truffly, sweet berries, satin texture. Pair with truffled risotto.

Kitchen Survivor™ Grade: C

Your notes: _____

Cristom Mt. Jefferson Cuvee Pinot Noir,   **Pts**
Willamette Valley, Oregon 2008   **$29**   **93**

A crown jewel of Oregon Pinot that ages beautifully if you can resist the urge to open it. That's not easy because the dusty-smoky, red licorice and cocoa style make this wine delicious in youth, especially when paired with game birds, lamb, and mushroom dishes.

Kitchen Survivor™ Grade: B+

Your notes: _____

Domaine Drouhin (*droo-AHN*)   **Pts**
Willamette Valley Pinot Noir,   **$40**   **90**
Oregon 2008

Always subtle and tightly wound, so you should decant this wine to unlock the layers: dark plum, cherry liqueur, cocoa and a gamy truffle note. Pair with mushroom risotto or braised lamb shanks.

Kitchen Survivor™ Grade: B+

Domaine Serene Evenstad Reserve Pinot   **Pts**
Noir, Willamette Valley, Oregon 2007   **$65**   **91**
Pie cherry, pomegranate, sweet vanilla and smoke!
This wine cellars nicely, and to pair it, (young or old),
let the wine's acidity play off a rich duck confit or a
rabbit stew, to tease out the spice and tobacco notes.
Kitchen Survivor™ Grade: B+
Your notes: _____

Penfolds Cellar Reserve Pinot Noir   **Pts**
Adelaide Hills, Australia 2007   **$44**   **92**
Fragrant and earthy, with dark cherry, spice and beet-
root notes and a smoky grip that's fantastic with
smoked pork or duck confit with a cherry reduction.
Kitchen Survivor™ Grade: B+
Your notes: _____

Ponzi Pinot Noir, Willamette Valley,   **Pts**
Oregon 2008   **$35**   **89**
Ponzi is always elegant and perfumey. This bottling
shows violets, delicate spice, floral and sweet cherry
notes that really open up with aeration. A mushroom
and herb pasta will bring out the earthy notes.
Kitchen Survivor™ Grade: C
Your notes: _____

Sokol-Blosser Dundee Hills Pinot Noir,   **Pts**
Willamette Valley, Oregon 2007   **$38**   **92**
The best yet from S-B and that's sayin' somethin'. I
love the laser-pure cherry fruit, campfire smoke and
potpourri notes, and the pure satin texture. A fantas-
tic match with wood-grilled salmon.
Kitchen Survivor™ Grade: B+
Your notes: _____

Willamette Valley Vineyards Founder's   **Pts**
Reserve Pinot Noir, Oregon 2007   **$25**   **88**
An affordable reserve that delivers: juicy red cherry,
cola and wet stone notes, and a sleek texture; pairs
perfectly with tender veal or rare-grilled salmon.
Kitchen Survivor™ Grade: B+
Your notes: _____

TOP TEN PINOT NOIRS:
FRENCH RED BURGUNDY

Domaine Albert Bichot Mercurey,   **Pts**
Burgundy, France 2009   **$24**   **90**
Lots of savory smoke, white pepper, cumin and cranberry notes, framed by soft vanilla scents from oak aging. A Delta pick with pedigree and style that will match pastas, fish, meat dishes and fine cheeses.
Kitchen Survivor™ Grade: B
Your notes: _____

Domaine Joblot Givry Cellier aux Moines   **Pts**
Burgundy, France 2007   **$42**   **90**
Givry offers great terroir for the money: dark cherry fruit, anise, mushroomy notes and a satiny texture with subtle chalky grip. It's a great match for slow-cooker stews or silky-smoky rare-grilled salmon.
Kitchen Survivor™ Grade: B
Your notes: _____

Domaine Daniel Rion Nuits St. Georges   **Pts**
Grandes Vignes, Burgundy, France 2007   **$49**   **90**
Rion is a "banker" name for quality. This wine's dark berries, plums, touch of anise and hint of vanilla, carried on a frame of firm acidity and gentle tannins, make it a great match for roast duck or pork loin.
Kitchen Survivor™ Grade: B
Your notes: _____

Joseph Drouhin Cote de Beaune,   **Pts**
Burgundy, France 2007   **$36**   **91**
This has lovely wet stone earthiness and tangy cranberry-spice flavor that are feather-light on the tongue but long on the finish. It is a super match for a salad of beets and tangy goat cheese, or a light herb pasta.
Kitchen Survivor™ Grade: B+
Your notes: _____

Joseph Faiveley Gevrey Chambertin,   **Pts**
Burgundy, France 2008   **$55**   **91**
A great expression of Gevrey terroir: lavender, smoke, cardamom and dark cherry notes, with grippy tannins that mean the wine is built for the cellar. Pair with roast duck or quail, or the classic coq au vin.

Your notes: _____

Joseph Faiveley Mercurey Clos des Myglands, Burgundy, France 2008

$29   Pts 89

Layers of smoky-dusty earth, red currant and cranberry fruit, plus a hint of white pepper spice in the finish, make this a great partner for an earthy-bacon-y bean stew or a cheesy leek-and-potato gratin.

Kitchen Survivor™ Grade: B+

Your notes: _____

Louis Latour Marsannay, Burgundy, France 2007

$17   Pts 88

The delicate and charming side of Burgundy, with smoke, cranberries and red currants and a spicy blood orange flavor in the finish. Pair it with ratatouille!

Kitchen Survivor™ Grade: B

Your notes: _____

Louis Jadot Beaune Clos des Ursules, Burgundy, France 2007

$55   Pts 93

This is a monopole (wholly-owned single vineyard) for which Jadot is justly famous. It is tangy and smoky, with blood orange and red cherry fruit and bewitching spices. Worthy of a wild mushroom or truffle feast!

Kitchen Survivor™ Grade: A+

Your notes: _____

Marquis d'Angerville Volnay, Burgundy, France 2007

$50   Pts 94

Talk about terroir: sundried tomato and wood smoke, lapsang souchong tea and consomme, silky cherries through to the finish. Pair with mushroom dishes.

Kitchen Survivor™ Grade: A+

Your notes: _____

Nicolas Potel Savigny-les-Beaune, Burgundy, France 2007

$40   Pts 91

A great combo of exuberant black cherry fruit and smoky earth, that's unmistakably Burgundy. The plump texture with a hint of chalky grip makes it pleasant now to pair with mild cheeses like Beaufort, or slow-braised pork or chicken. Will age 5-7 years.

Kitchen Survivor™ Grade: B

Your notes: _____

Italian Reds

Category Profile: Remember the days when "Chianti" meant those kitschy straw-covered bottles? Tuscany's signature red has come a long way in quality since then, pulling much of the Italian wine world with it. But let me clear up some understandable confusion about the labels and styles. As quality has improved, Chianti has "morphed" into three tiers of wine—varietal Sangiovese (*san-joe-VAY-zay*), labeled with the grape name; traditional Chianti in a range of styles; and the luxury tier, which includes top regional wines like Brunello, and the so-called Super Tuscan reds (see below). Many of the major Tuscan wineries produce wines in all three categories. The basic Sangioveses largely populate the budget price tier, and some offer good value. (Most are, in my opinion, just "red wine" without a lot of character.) Chianti itself now spans the entire price and quality spectrum from budget quaff to boutique collectible, with the top-quality *classico* and *riserva* versions worthy of aging in the cellar. Finally, the Super Tuscans emerged because wineries wanted creative license to use international grapes outside the traditional Chianti "recipe" (and, I guess, with fantasy names like Summus, Sassicaia, and Luce, poetic license, too!). What they all have in common is that Italian "zest"—savory rustic spice in the scent, plus vibrant acidity—and international sophistication from the use of French oak barrels for aging and some French grapes (like Cab and Merlot) for blending. The wines are often cellar worthy and nearly always pricey—I've listed the deals in this section.

I have also included the rest of the world of Italian red wines, including the great wines of the Piedmont district, and many interesting emerging regional wines. These are often some of the best deals in red wine, period, and almost always very food-friendly, so check them out.

Serve: Cool room temperature (the budget-priced wines are generally nice with a light chill); the "bigger" wines—classicos, riservas, Super Tuscans, and Barolos—benefit from aeration (pour into the glass and swirl or decant into a pitcher or carafe with plenty of air space).

When: Any food occasion, from snack to supper to celebration.

With: Almost anything; truthfully, nearly every wine in this section warrants the "Food Friendly" symbol. Especially great wherever tomato sauce, cheese, olive oil, or savory herbs (rosemary, basil, oregano, sage) are present.

In: The One™ glass for red or a larger-bowled red wineglass.

Almost Top Ten Italian Reds:

These wines are also well worth checking out.

Pio Cesare Barolo
Morgante Nero d'Avola
Marchesi di Barolo Cannubi
Solengo
Cappezzana Carmignano & Ghiaie della Furba

"Worth the splurge":

Arnaldo Caprai Montefalco Sagrantino
Masseto
Angelo Gaja Barbaresco
Scavino Barolo
Dal Forno Romano Amarone
Quintarelli Fiore Rosso

TOP TEN ITALIAN REDS: $25 OR LESS

Avignonesi Rosso di Montepulciano, Tuscany, Italy 2009   **$18**   **Pts 90**

This is the Sangiovese grape? Surely one of the most ripe and heady versions ever, with dark berry, anise and savory cured meat notes. The fruit pops even more when you pair it with a creamy fresh pecorino.
Kitchen Survivor™ Grade: B
Your notes: _____

Badia a Coltibuono Chianti Classico, Tuscany, Italy 2007   **$25**   **Pts 89**

Traditional-style Chianti Classico with centuries of pedigree. The strawberry and red licorice notes on a chalky-taut frame are built for food. Pair with a cheesy tomato-y pasta or caprese salad.
Kitchen Survivor™ Grade: B+
Your notes: _____

Castello di Gabbiano Chianti Classico, Tuscany, Italy 2007   **$13**   **Pts 88**

This soft, light Chianti, is all red berries, plums and savory black pepper and coriander spice. Pair it with cured meats, olive tapenade or sausage pizza.
Kitchen Survivor™ Grade: B+
Your notes: _____

Dievole Chianti Classico Vendemmia, Tuscany, Italy 2007   **$19**   **Pts 90**

This Chianti competes on quality and finesse with the "super-Chiantis" that cost twice as much. Layers of juicy strawberry with notes of white pepper, sweet herbs and coriander make it a snappy savory mouthful - delicious with a sausage and pepper panini.
Kitchen Survivor™ Grade: B+
Your notes: _____

Falesco Vitiano (*fuh-LESS-co vee-tee-AH-no*), Umbria, Italy 2009   **$12**   **Pts 89**

A full-blooded blend of Sangiovese, Merlot and Cab that bursts with dark jammy fruit: plums, cherries and blackberry. Pizza- priced, but good enough for gourmet food - the best risotto or pasta you can muster.

Kitchen Survivor™ Grade: B
Your notes: _____

Frescobaldi Nipozzano Chianti Rufina Riserva, Tuscany, Italy 2007 — $25 — Pts 91

Luxuriant dark plum fruit and anise with a hint of tarry black olive and a grip of tannin - it all adds up to the perfect partner for sausage and olive pizza.

Kitchen Survivor™ Grade: B+
Your notes: _____

Marchesi di Gresy Monte Aribaldo Dolcetto d'Alba, Piedmont, Italy 2007 — $17 — Pts 89

If you want a dance partner for your tongue (and your plate) this wine is ready to cut in on your boring everyday dinner vino. It's solidly old world with an inky, tarry, violet fragrance and very savory, spicy plum and balsamic palate, all on a sprightly, soft frame.

Kitchen Survivor™ Grade: B+
Your notes: _____

Michele Chiarlo Barbera d'Asti 'Le Orme', Italy 2007 — $15 — Pts 90

A lot of Italian character for the money! The lively acidity and flavor of cherry liqueur, and balsamic lingers into the finish and gets even better with aeration. Pair with a rich sage-prosciutto pasta or piave cheese.

Kitchen Survivor™ Grade: B+
Your notes: _____

Taurino Salice Salentino Rosso Riserva, Apulia, Italy 2007 — $12 — Pts 89

Rustic, mouth-watering, characterful - juicy dark berries, meat stock and peppered figs. On that note, pair it with prosciutto-wrapped figs with balsamic.

Kitchen Survivor™ Grade: B+
Your notes: _____

Vietti Barbera d'Asti Tre Vigne, Piedmont, Italy 2008 — $17 — Pts 89

Juicy and fresh, with scents of tangy raspberry and an earthy note of ink and graphite. The fruit pops even more when paired with a creamy-mild cheese such as fresh Pecorino or some buttery gnocchi with sage.

Kitchen Survivor™ Grade: A+
Your notes: _____

TOP TEN ITALIAN REDS:
OVER $25

Badia a Coltibuono Sangioveto,   **Pts**
Tuscany, Italy 2003   **$60**   **90**

A classical Sangiovese-based super Tuscan with lots
of leather and herb complexity, deep dark cherry fruit
and impressive ageability for the price.

Kitchen Survivor™ Grade: B+

Your notes: _____

Castelgiocondo Brunello di Montalcino,   **Pts**
(Frescobaldi) Tuscany, Italy 2005   **$52**   **90**

While intended for aging, this wine shows complex
layers of cocoa, charcoal, black figs and sassafras
spice, even in youth. Decant it for aeration and pair
with a well-marbled steak slathered with basil pesto.

Kitchen Survivor™ Grade: B+

Your notes: _____

Castellare di Castellina Chianti Classico   **Pts**
Riserva, Tuscany, Italy 2007   **$28**   **90**

A very special Chianti Classico, redolent of sassafras,
licorice, leather and dark plum fruit, with a savory-
spicy finish tailor-made for a garlicky, herb-y stew.

Kitchen Survivor™ Grade: A+

Your notes: _____

Castello di Ama Chianti Classico,   **Pts**
Tuscany, Italy 2007   **$36**   **92**

Old world without being austere, and a true rendition
of traditional-style Chianti. That means sweet strawberry fruit, heady red licorice, black pepper and
cumin with silky tannins and a spicy-leathery finish.
Pair with garlicky leg of lamb or basil pesto pasta.

Kitchen Survivor™ Grade: A

Your notes: _____

Ceretto Zonchera Barolo DOCG   **Pts**
Piedmont, Italy 2005   **$51**   **91**

Tar, rose potpourri, Japanese plums and licorice, and
it will only get better with time. Tame the tannin
with a rich cheesy risotto, buttery pasta, or slow-
cooked wine-braised meat.

Kitchen Survivor™ Grade: B

Your notes: _____

Marchese Antinori Chianti Classico Riserva,   Pts
Tuscany, Italy 2007 $35   89

Lots of old-world, classic Chianti character here: strawberry fruit leather, savory herbs, black olive and peppery spice. Serve with smoked pork chops.

Kitchen Survivor™ Grade: B+

Your notes: _____

Marchesi di Gresy Barbaresco Martinenga,   Pts
Piedmont, Italy 2006 $60   92

Taut cherry licorice and tangy-sassafras notes in scent lead to dark plums and heady hoisin flavors on the palate. Pair with a big steak with sauteed mushrooms to tame the tannin and tease out the wine's potential.

Kitchen Survivor™ Grade: B+

Your notes: _____

Ruffino Chianti Classico Riserva   Pts
Ducale (*doo-CALL-eh*) Oro (Gold $40   91
Label), Tuscany, Italy 2006

Although it's pricey, this classic delivers leathery, peppered fig and balsamic in layer after layer of complexity. Pair it with fresh figs with black pepper, balsamic and burrata (or fresh mozzarella) cheese.

Kitchen Survivor™ Grade: A+

Your notes: _____

Val di Suga Brunello di Montalcino,   Pts
Tuscany, Italy 2004 $66   94

A steal for great Brunello, and a find for its delicious drinkability. Serve some slow-braised short ribs to unlock the lusty layers: leather, chewy dark cherry, smoke, spice and anise. Buy some extra for the cellar.

Kitchen Survivor™ Grade: A

Your notes: _____

Val di Suga Rosso di Montalcino,   Pts
Tuscany, Italy 2006 $26   91

"Baby Brunello," meaning it's made from younger vines, drinkable younger, and less expensive. Handsdown the most complex Rosso I have ever tasted: vanilla, coffee, ripe & dusky plum fruit, chalky finish.

Kitchen Survivor™ Grade: A

Your notes: _____

TOP TEN SUPER TUSCANS

Castello Banfi Cum Laude Super Tuscan,   **Pts**
Tuscany, Italy 2006   **$35**   **89**

Spicy, plummy and tarry, with dried spices, heady herbs and a licorice note. It's a great value for the complexity, and very food friendly. Pair with rich meat stews or slow-braised short ribs or lamb shanks.
Kitchen Survivor™ Grade: B+

Your notes: _____

Castello di Gabbiano Alleanza,   **Pts**
Tuscany, Italy 2007   **$35**   **93**

The layers of licorice, vanilla bean, plum and sweet spices with a nice chalky grip are stunningly complex when paired with sage rubbed pork or a veal chop. Why pay more for Super Tuscan? This one's got it all.
Kitchen Survivor™ Grade: A+

Your notes: _____

Guado Al Tasso Red Blend, Bolgheri,   **Pts**
Tuscany, Italy 2006   **$115**   **95**

French grapes in a Tuscan style: taut red fruits, fragrant floral-herbaceousness and chalky tannins, plus sweet vanilla and cedar-smokiness. A great match for rosemary lamb or fresh pecorino cheese.
Kitchen Survivor™ Grade: B+

Your notes: _____

La Vite Lucente, Tuscany,   **Pts**
Italy 2007   **$25**   **91**

Unmistakably Tuscan with its dried spice, wet clay and red cherry scents, lively acidity and chalky texture. The vivid berry on the palate, delivers both juiciness and finesse. Pair with spaghetti Bolognese.
Kitchen Survivor™ Grade: A+

Your notes: _____

Luce della Vite Super Tuscan, Tuscany,   **Pts**
Italy 2006   **$80**   **94**

One of the great Super Tuscans! It's a minty-spicy blend of Merlot and Sangiovese, with rosemary and cedar notes and luscious red fruits on the palate. Pair with a top-quality grilled steak or pesto pasta.
Kitchen Survivor™ Grade: A+

Your notes: _____

Ornellaia Super Tuscan, Bolgheri,   **Pts**
Tuscany, Italy 2006   **$125**   **93**

Elegant, cedary and Bordeaux-like, with dense cassis fruit, cinnamon spice, vanilla and dusty-leafy crushed mint. The Tuscan touch adds chalky texture and vivid acidity. Pair with Tuscan steak or basil pesto.
Kitchen Survivor™ Grade: B+
Your notes: _____

Solaia (Antinori), Tuscany,   **Pts**
Italy 2007   **$270**   **97**

It's a Super Tuscan in a luxury Bordeaux style: dark berry, cassis and fig fruit, dark chocolate, sweet spice, vanilla and a whiff of violets. The palate is velvety and smoky, with sumptuous cassis fruit and a layered dusty cedar and rosemary finish. Pair with steak.
Kitchen Survivor™ Grade: A
Your notes: _____

Tenuta del Terriccio Tassinaia,   **Pts**
Tuscany, Italy 2006   **$35**   **90**

The cedary Cab shows in this Super Tuscan blend with Merlot and Sangiovese. The taut acidity, grippy tannin, and deep core of blackberry and red cherry fruit are impeccably balanced. Pair with osso buco.
Kitchen Survivor™ Grade: A
Your notes: _____

Tenuta Sette Ponti Crognolo,   **Pts**
Tuscany, Italy 2008   **$35**   **92**

A savory pipe tobacco-strawberry-licorice-scented blend of Sangiovese and Merlot that serves up coriander and cardamom spices with aeration. Pair with pasta with sausage and herbs or cheesy gnocchi.
Kitchen Survivor™ Grade: A
Your notes: _____

Tignanello, Tuscany,   **Pts**
Italy 2007   **$95**   **95**

A "Super Tuscan" true to it Sangiovese roots. That character shows as red fruits (cherry, cranberry, strawberry) with soft sassafras and gamy notes, and a bewitching floral-anise fragrance. Pair with prosciutto, garlic and sage pasta or pesto-slathered steak.
Kitchen Survivor™ Grade: A
Your notes: _____

Merlot

Grape Profile: I have bemoaned the flood of so-so Merlot began to deluge the market, after publicity of the so-called French Paradox made the connection to the mass market of moderate red wine consumption with heart health. The news remains good when it comes to the health benefits of wine consumption (in moderation), but not so on Merlot quality. In my tastings for last year's guide I thought things were improving but this year proved me wrong. Merlot is still a maddeningly under-performing category, with a majority of widely-available bottlings falling short in quality and character. The selections in this section are the worthy ones.

As with other market-leading varietals like Chardonnay and Cabernet Sauvignon, Merlot can range both in price, from budget to boutique, and in complexity, from soft and simple to "serious." Across the spectrum, Merlot is modeled on the wines from its home region of Bordeaux, France. At the basic level, that means medium body and soft texture, with nice plum and berry fruit flavor.

The more ambitious versions have more body, tannin, and fruit concentration and usually a good bit of oakiness in the scent and taste. Washington State, California's Sonoma and Napa regions, and Chile are my favorite growing regions for varietal Merlot. Most Merlot producers follow the Bordeaux practice of blending in some Cabernet Sauvignon (or another of the classic Bordeaux red grapes) to complement and enhance the wines' taste and complexity.

Serve: *Cool* room temperature.

When: With meals, of course; and the basic bottlings are soft enough to enjoy on their own as a cocktail alternative.

With: Anything with which you enjoy red wine, especially cheeses, roasts, fuller-bodied fish, and grilled foods.

In: The One™ glass for red, or a larger-bowled red wine stem.

MERLOT'S KISSING COUSINS: If you are looking for something different but similar to Merlot, check out two South American specialties. First, there's Argentina's Malbec (*MAHL-beck*), a red grape originally from Bordeaux. It's similar in body and smoothness to Merlot, with lots of smoky aromatic complexity. Some wineries to look for: Salentein, Navarro Correas, Catena, Trapiche, Terrazas and Argento. Second, from Chile, try Carmenere (*car-muh-NAIR-eh*), also a Bordeaux import that was originally misidentified as Merlot in many Chilean vineyards. Its smooth texture and plum fruit are complemented by an exotically meaty-smoky scent. Look for Carmeneres from Concha y Toro, Mont-Gras, Arboleda, Casa Lapostolle and Veramonte Primus. Check out "Uncommon Reds" for more on these.

Almost Top Ten Merlots:

These wines are also well worth checking out.

Swanson
Wente Crane Ridge
Pine Ridge Crimson Creek
Franciscan
Truchard
Casa Lapostolle Cuvee Alexandre

TOP TEN MERLOT VALUES: $25 OR LESS

(See also Top Ten Bordeaux for Merlot-based wines)

Chateau St. Jean Merlot,   **Pts**
Sonoma, California 2007   **$25**   **91**
Hits all the prettiest notes that Merlot is capable of - dark berry, plum, violets and smoky-tarriness, with a are long silky finish. Pair with a velvety prime rib.
Kitchen Survivor™ Grade: B+

Your notes: _____

Chateau Ste. Michelle Indian Wells Merlot,   **Pts**
Columbia Valley, Washington 2008   **$18** **91**
This has the sumptuous black fruit and soft, velvety richness that Merlot is *supposed* to have, plus a lovely dusty-cocoa finish. Pair with cheeses, pork roast with a fig stuffing, or dark chocolate.
Kitchen Survivor™ Grade: B+

Your notes: _____

Clos du Bois North Coast Merlot,   **Pts**
California 2007   **$17**   **89**
I am SO thrilled that this hugely popular wine has busted out of its quality doldrums. This vintage has lush plummy fruit kissed with cedar, for a great price. Pair with blue cheese burgers or mom's meatloaf.
Kitchen Survivor™ Grade: C

Your notes: _____

Columbia Crest Grand Estates Merlot,   **Pts**
Columbia Valley, Washington 2008   **$10** **87**
The most reliable budget Merlot and a "house red" no-brainer for its soft plum fruit with a touch of earthiness. Bring on any dinner, this will match it!
Kitchen Survivor™ Grade: C

Your notes: _____

Fetzer Valley Oaks Merlot,   **Pts**
California 2008   **$9**   **86**
One of the best basic California Merlots out there, with juicy berry flavors and a good survivor grade that makes it a great "house wine" for everyday meals.
Kitchen Survivor™ Grade: A

Your notes: _____

Ravenswood Vintners Blend
Merlot, California 2008 $10   Pts
                                                  89
You can't do better for $10 than this plummy and
juicy gulper; it's even better than the signature Zin.
Kitchen Survivor™ Grade: B
Your notes: _____

Raymond Reserve Merlot, Napa,   Pts
California 2006 $24   90
Here is a reserve that earns the accolade and does the
grape proud. Sweet baking spices and blueberry-
plum fruit are like a county fair-winning pie without
the sugar. The palate is dusty and smoky. The price,
for this quality, is a gift! Serve with pork tenderloin.
Kitchen Survivor™ Grade: A
Your notes: _____

Sebastiani Sonoma County   Pts
Merlot, California 2007 $17   90
So much CA Merlot pleasure for the money: deep
wild-berry fruit layered with tarragon, tobacco, vanilla
and dark chocolate notes that linger in the long finish.
At this price, it's a gift. Delicious on its own, but
Piave cheese is the perfect, decadent pairing.
Kitchen Survivor™ Grade: B
Your notes: _____

Souverain Alexander   Pts
Valley Merlot, California 2007 $19   90
You get a lot for the money: sweet plum, dusty cocoa
and tangy cured meat notes on the palate, plus a long
smoky finish. A nice match for a wintry pot roast.
Kitchen Survivor™ Grade: B
Your notes: _____

Sterling Vineyards Merlot, Napa   Pts
California 2007 $22   89
The brand that put Merlot on the Napa map is now
back on the quality map - yay! It's all black plums
and dark berries, with coffee bean and charry-dusty
scents and flavors. Pair with dark chocolate.
Kitchen Survivor™ Grade: B+
Your notes: _____

TOP TEN MERLOTS:
OVER $25

Beringer Bancroft Ranch Merlot, Howell   **Pts**
Mountain, Napa Valley, California 2006   **$75**   **97**

One of Napa's greatest Merlots, luxuriant with chocolate, blueberry, plum, wet stone and autumn leaf-pile notes. Truly meant for aging, and for pairing with prime steak, pesto pasta or lamb chops.

Kitchen Survivor™ Grade: C

Your notes: _____

Duckhorn Napa Merlot, Napa,   **Pts**
California 2007   **$46**   **92**

This is the benchmark, unwavering in its plummy-dusty, velvety style kissed with vanilla, dark cocoa and a touch of cedar. A great match for braised shortribs.

Kitchen Survivor™ Grade: B+

Your notes: _____

Frog's Leap Merlot, Rutherford,   **Pts**
Napa Valley, California 2007   **$34**   **91**

Figs with black pepper and chocolate shavings - how's that sound? Tastes even better thanks to the licorice, vanilla and coffee bean notes in the mid-palate and long finish. Pair it with mushroom risotto.

Kitchen Survivor™ Grade: B

Your notes: _____

Grgich Hills Estate Merlot, Napa,   **Pts**
California 2006   **$42**   **92**

A whiff of old world, slaty-graphite earthiness distinguishes Grgich among top Napa Merlots. Pair with a roast to showcase the lush dark plum and cassis fruit.

Kitchen Survivor™ Grade: B

Your notes: _____

L'Ecole No. 41 Seven Hills Vineyard Estate   **Pts**
Merlot, Walla Walla, Washington 2007   **$36**   **91**

This label was an early indicator of the potential for Merlot in the Walla Walla region. It remains a benchmark, offering so much chocolatey-dark cherry depth of fruit for the money. Rich and ripe enough to pair with chocolate. Great with spiced pork or duck.

Kitchen Survivor™ Grade: B

Your notes: _____

Newton Unfiltered Merlot
Napa, California 2006

Pts

$50   91

Sweet pipe tobacco, wet gravel and dark plum notes, all delivered with subtlety, add up to a complex old world-style that's lovely with a simple steak au poivre or chicken roasted with black olives.

Kitchen Survivor™ *Grade: C*

Your notes: _____

Northstar Walla Walla Merlot,
Columbia Valley, Washington 2006

Pts

$40   93

This wine bursts with plum and dark cherry liqueur flavors, while maintaining subtlety and layers of smoke, cocoa, and dusty-leafiness in the very long finish. Super now, and I suspect it will age very well.

Kitchen Survivor™ *Grade: A*

Your notes: _____

St. Clement Merlot, Napa,
California 2007

Pts

$28   94

A true unsung hero on the Napa reds landscape, and that is why the price is a steal for this quality. The complex pencil lead, vanilla-cinnamon scents and deeply textured, lush plum compote flavor. Gorgeous with pesto or slow-braised lamb shanks.

Kitchen Survivor™ *Grade: B+*

Your notes: _____

Shafer Napa Merlot,
California 2007

Pts

$46   92

Dark cocoa- and cream-topped berries and plums cloaked in velvet! Need I say more? Well yes: pair with blue cheese burgers or dark chocolate.

Kitchen Survivor™ *Grade: B*

Your notes: _____

Silverado Merlot Napa
Valley, California 2007

Pts

$35   90

I love the earthy-brambly wild berry notes underpinned with an old world-style dusty-herbaceous note. That makes it great for earthy foods like roasted eggplant, grilled Portabella mushrooms or lentil soup.

Kitchen Survivor™ *Grade: B*

Your notes: _____

Cabernet Sauvignon & Blends

Grape Profile: Although Merlot ranks above it, Cabernet Sauvignon remains a top-selling red varietal wine. It grows well virtually all over the wine world and gives good to excellent quality and flavor at every price level, from steal to splurge. Its style can vary, based on the wine's quality level, from uncomplicated everyday styles to the super-intense boutique bottlings. The most famous and plentiful sources of Cabernet are Bordeaux in France, California (especially Sonoma and Napa), Washington State, and Italy on the high end with its Super Tuscan versions; and I think Chile shines in the low- to mid-priced category. Classically, it has a scent and taste of dark berries (black cherry, blackberry), plus notes of spice, earth, cocoa, cedar, and even mint that can be very layered and complex in the best wines. It has medium to very full body and often more tannin—that bit of a tongue-gripping sensation that one of my waiters once described, perfectly I think, as "a slipcover for the tongue, ranging from terry cloth to suede to velvet," depending on the wine in question. Oakiness, either a little or a lot depending on the growing region and price category, is also a common Cabernet feature. Combined, these can make for a primo mouthful of wine, which surely explains why Cabernet is king of collectible wines.

A note about blends: As described previously for Merlot, Cabernet Sauvignon wines often follow the Bordeaux blending model, with one or more of the traditional Bordeaux red grapes—Merlot, Cabernet Franc, Petit Verdot, and Malbec—blended in for balance and complexity. Australia pioneered blending Cabernet Sauvignon with Shiraz—a delicious combination that the wine buying market has embraced. Those blends are listed either here or in the Shiraz section, according to which of the two grapes is dominant in the blend (it will be listed first on the label, too).

Serve: Cool room temperature; the fuller-bodied styles benefit from aeration—pour into the glass a bit ahead of time or decant into a carafe (but if you forget, don't sweat it; if you care to, swirling the glass does help).

When: With your favorite red wine meals, but the every-day bottlings are soft enough for cocktail-hour sipping.

With: Anything you'd serve alongside a red; especially complements beef, lamb, goat cheese and hard cheeses, pesto sauce, and dishes scented with basil, rosemary, sage, or oregano.

In: The One™ glass for red or a larger-bowled red wineglass.

Almost Top Ten Cabernets/Cab blends:

These wines are also well worth checking out.

Concha y Toro Marques de Casa Concha
St. Supery Dollarhide Ranch
Gallo Frey Ranch
Franciscan
Simi
Kathryn Hall
Stonestreet
Opus One
Quintessa

Emerging, and "Worth the Splurge"

Three Sticks
Stuhlmuller
Cardinale
Seven Stones
Gargiulo
Darioush
Hestan
Rocca Family
Stephanie
Dana Estate

Clos du Bois Sonoma Cabernet   **Pts**
Sauvignon, California 2008   **$14**   **88**

Although the Merlot is far more popular, I think the wild berry, cedar, mint and anise character of this wine makes it the true Clos du Bois calling card. Pair with charred steaks or earthy black bean stew.
Kitchen Survivor™ Grade: C

Your notes: _____

Baron Philippe de Rothschild,   **Pts**
Escudo Rojo Cabernet Blend, Chile 2007   **$14**   **91**

It's REALLY worth the search for this heady glassful: super-sweet dark berry fruit woven through with savory cumin and beef stock notes. Pair with chicken mole poblano, pork chile verde, or lamb brochettes.
Kitchen Survivor™ Grade: B+

Your notes: _____

Jacob's Creek Reserve Cabernet   **Pts**
Sauvignon, Australia 2008   **$12**   **91**

Exotic crushed mint and blackberry notes and a succulent juiciness make this wine perfect to pair with your lustiest grill fare - big burgers or barbecued ribs.
Kitchen Survivor™ Grade: B

Your notes: _____

Los Vascos Cabernet Sauvignon,   **Pts**
Chile 2008   **$10**   **90**

This has more cedary-dusty, blackberry, bay leaf and leather varietal character than many Cabs twice the price. Pair with slow-cooker stews or Piave cheese.
Kitchen Survivor™ Grade: B

Your notes: _____

Louis Martini Sonoma Cabernet   **Pts**
Sauvignon, California 2007   **$16**   **89**

A juicy mouthful of velvety wild berries, bramble, tar and dust - lots for the money from a classic California name. Pair it with juicy burgers or steak au poivre.
Kitchen Survivor™ Grade: C

Your notes: _____

Ravenswood Vintners Blend   Pts
Cabernet Sauvignon, California 2008 $10   89

Real dusty-coffee bean Cab character like this for $10 is all too rare. The juicy blackberry fruit and smooth mouthfeel are tailor-made for beef stew.

Kitchen Survivor™ Grade: B

Your notes: _____

Rosemount Diamond Label   Pts
Cabernet Sauvignon Australia 2009 $10   88

Jammy, juicy, easy-drinking and a great price - how's that for a great "house red" candidate? A great red for everyday dinners, from pastrami paninis to meatloaf.

Kitchen Survivor™ Grade: C

Your notes: _____

Santa Rita 120 Cabernet Sauvignon,   Pts
Rapel Valley, Chile 2009 $8   89

What an amazing Cab deal. Tons of soft blackberry fruit and a dusty cumin scent. Pair with grilled hanger steak, burgers, chicken, or mushrooms.

Kitchen Survivor™ Grade: C

Your notes: _____

Sebastiani Sonoma Cabernet   Pts
Sauvignon, California 2007 $16   91

Lots of Cab character for the price! The wild berry-brambly fruit, allspice notes, savory herbs and sassafras are great with jerk pork or blackened chicken.

Kitchen Survivor™ Grade: B

Your notes: _____

Veramonte Cabernet Sauvignon,   Pts
Reserva, Colchagua Valley, Chile 2008 $13   90

The anise-wild berry flavors, grippy tannin, and savory spice and black olive notes taste like twice the price. Pair it with grilled eggplant and fennel sausages, or savory, saucy barbecue, anything with a smoky char.

Kitchen Survivor™ Grade: C

Your notes: _____

(See also Top Ten Cabernets: Napa $20-$40)

		Pts
Antu Ninquen Cabernet Sauvignon-Carmenere, Colchagua, Chile 2008	$22	93

Heady, smoky and spicy; bewitching cumin and consomme notes and ripe crushed plum fruit make this a perfect Delta pick to shine in-flight and pair well with anything from cheesy pastas to a velvety beef filet.
Kitchen Survivor™ Grade: A

Your notes: _____

		Pts
Beringer Knights Valley Cabernet Sauvignon, Sonoma, California 2007	$22	93

Greatness at a price you can swallow. Fragrant pipe tobacco, chocolate and coffee bean notes; luscious dark fruit, velvety tannins. Great with prime steak.
Kitchen Survivor™ Grade: A

Your notes: _____

		Pts
Catena Zapata Cabernet Sauvignon, Mendoza, Argentina 2007	$45	94

Argentina's blue chip Cab, showing the pen ink, violet and tar scents which to me are classic to Argentina. It's packed with deep dusty-cocoa and cassis. In Mendoza they'd pair it with local grass-fed beef!
Kitchen Survivor™ Grade: B+

Your notes: _____

		Pts
Cousino-Macul Antiguas Reservas Cabernet Sauvignon, Chile 2008	$22	90

Dusty tobacco, mushrooms, leather and dark berry fruit make this one of the most complex Chilean Cabs out there. I chose it for Delta for the great food versatility, and intensity that will shine out in-flight.
Kitchen Survivor™ Grade: B

Your notes: _____

		Pts
Chateau Ste. Michelle Indian Wells Cabernet Sauvignon, Columbia Vly, Washington 2008	$28	90

Sweet dark blueberry fruit and chocolate fudge flavors - irresistible with a juicy cheddar burger, huh?
Kitchen Survivor™ Grade: B

Your notes: _____

Chateau St. Jean Cabernet Sauvignon,   **Pts**
Sonoma, California 2006   **$27**   **92**

Fantastic varietal character - blackcurrant, cedar, roasted coffee and autumn leaves. Pair with pesto to bring out the layers of pencil dust and dark cherry.
Kitchen Survivor™ Grade: B

Your notes: _____

Clos du Bois Reserve Cabernet Sauvignon,   **Pts**
Alexander Valley, California 2007   **$22**   **91**

A "reserve" that earns the billing is rare. At this price the wine is a gift of succulent wild berry fruit, anise and vanilla perfume, with structure and length. Pair with barbecued salmon, prime steak or rich cheeses.
Kitchen Survivor™ Grade: B

Your notes: _____

Louis Martini Alexander Valley Cabernet   **Pts**
Sauvignon Reserve, California 2007   **$32**   **91**

The fig and blackberry fruit are lavished with coconut-scented oak, yet underneath is a brambly savoriness that keeps it balanced and built for a meal with pumped-up flavors: rosemary rack of lamb, anyone?
Kitchen Survivor™ Grade: B+

Your notes: _____

Penfolds Bin 389 Cabernet Shiraz,   **Pts**
South Australia 2007   **$37**   **97**

I am not the tattoo type but if I were, I might consider the digits "389". The wine makes a similarly indelible impression: powerful and impeccably balanced, with black fig and coconut sweetness keeping time with balsamic, cedar and black olive notes. Cellar, or serve young with lamb shanks, cheeses, or dark chocolate.
Kitchen Survivor™ Grade: A+

Your notes: _____

Souverain Alexander Valley   **Pts**
Cabernet Sauvignon, California 2006   **$20**   **90**

Cab balance and elegance, defined. You get all the leafy-dusty, dark cassis fruit and sweet vanilla of classic CA Cab, without heaviness. Velvety, smooth and loooong. Pair with rosemary pork tenderloin.
Kitchen Survivor™ Grade: B

Your notes: _____

TOP TEN CABERNETS:
NEW WORLD ABOVE $45

Chalk Hill Estate Cabernet Sauvignon,   **Pts**
Chalk Hill, Sonoma, California 2007   **$70**   **97**
So opulent, and yet structured for cellaring. The luxuriant chocolate-dipped fig flavors are indulgent without being over-the-top. Manchego cheese lets the fruit shine out; or try it with velvety duck breast.
Kitchen Survivor™ Grade: A
Your notes: _____

Chateau St. Jean Cinq Cepages   **Pts**
Cabernet Blend, Sonoma California 2006   **$75**   **90**
Needs aeration to show its classic suppleness and layers of pencil lead, tobacco, cedar and dark cherry. Great with mustard- and herb-crusted rack of lamb.
Kitchen Survivor™ Grade: B+
Your notes: _____

Col Solare Red Blend, Columbia Valley,   **Pts**
Washington 2007   **$55**   **91**
This WA classic mix of Cab, Merlot and Cab Franc is shows new world dark berry and sweet anise and spice notes, and old world leafy-dusty tannins. Pair with butter and sage pasta or pork chile verde.
Kitchen Survivor™ Grade: B+
Your notes: _____

Concha y Toro Don Melchor Cabernet   **Pts**
Cabernet Sauvignon Reserva, Maipo, Chile 2007 **$70**   **91**
This wine is all espresso, lead pencil and blackberry elegance, with a smoothness in youth that belies its ability to cellar well for 10 years or more. Pair with tender meats like osso buco, or mushroom risotto.
Kitchen Survivor™ Grade: A
Your notes: _____

Jordan Cabernet Sauvignon, Alexander   **Pts**
Valley, California 2006   **$50**   **89**
There's huge fan club for this wine's elegant leafy-earthy, mint-and-plums style. Ages well in top years. Pair with grilled duck breast or herbed lamb loin.
Kitchen Survivor™ Grade: B
Your notes: _____

Justin Isosceles Cabernet Blend,   **Pts**
Paso Robles, California 2007   **$62**   **93**

This wine put Paso Robles on the map, and now stands with the big boys of Cab in Napa and Sonoma. Brambly black plum, molasses, black olive, sassafras and ginseng notes keep you thinking (and sipping!). Pair with Manchego cheese or steak au poivre.
Kitchen Survivor™ Grade: B+

Your notes: _____

Leonetti Cellar Cabernet Sauvignon,   **Pts**
Walla Walla, Washington 2007   **$85**   **94**

A long-time calling card of WA reds, for its depth and finesse. The wet gravel earthiness and chewy, brambly dark fruit lead to a long finish of smoky, cocoa elegance. Pair with grilled lamb chops or venison loin.
Kitchen Survivor™ Grade: A

Your notes: _____

Penfolds Bin 707 Cabernet Sauvignon,   **Pts**
South Australia 2007   **$140**   **98**

This wine cruises the spectrum of Cab flavors, from fudgy, cherry liqueur sweetness, to eucalyptus, mint, rosemary and sassafras. The concentration and velvety texture are delicious young, but the wine rewards aging with leather, consomme and truffle notes.
Kitchen Survivor™ Grade: A+

Your notes: _____

Rodney Strong Symmetry Meritage red   **Pts**
blend, Alexander Valley, California 2007 **$60** **92**

This wine's liquefied chamois texture is the perfect platform for the dense black fig, anise, sweet spice and coconut lavishness in the finish. Pair it with red wine-braised shortribs or aged goat cheese.
Kitchen Survivor™ Grade: B+

Your notes: _____

Silver Oak Alexander Valley   **Pts**
Cabernet Sauvignon, California 2006   **$70**   **91**

The signature brambly berry fruit with spice-coconut-dill scents from aging in American oak is lovely young, but the wine is also known for aging. Great with pasta Amatriciana (with Pecorino, bacon & tomato).
Kitchen Survivor™ Grade: B

Your notes: _____

Beaulieu Vineyard (BV) Rutherford   **Pts**
Cabernet Sauvignon, California 2007   **$26**   **90**

A rock-solid classic that earns the term. Dusty and layered, with autumn leaf, lead pencil, velvety dark berry and cedar spice through the finish. Pair with a great cheese or a rare-charred steak with 'shrooms.

Kitchen Survivor™ Grade: B+

Your notes: _____

Beringer Alluvium Red Blend,   **Pts**
Napa, California 2007   **$30**   **91**

Smoky earthiness and lush fig fruit - the perfect balance between old world elegance and new world fruit intensity. Pasta with Pecorino, mushrooms, prosciutto and sage brings out the layers beautifully.

Kitchen Survivor™ Grade: B+

Your notes: _____

Chappellet Signature Cabernet   **Pts**
Sauvignon, Napa, California 2007   **$42**   **94**

A velvet cloak for your tongue! And pure Napa Cab style--succulent blackcurrant fruit, minty-cedar notes and long, smoky finish. Delicious now, but the depth makes it a cellar candidate. Pair with smoked beef.

Kitchen Survivor™ Grade: B+

Your notes: _____

Faust Cabernet Sauvignon,   **Pts**
Napa Valley, California 2007   **$44**   **92**

A wonderfully complete wine that seems ready now and yet surely has the stuffing to age. I love the plush but firm tannin and deep core of blackberry-cedar flavors. Pair with basil pesto-slathered steak.

Kitchen Survivor™ Grade: B+

Your notes: _____

Flora Springs Cabernet Sauvignon,   **Pts**
Napa, California 2007   **$32**   **91**

So classically Napa but with a Bordeaux subtlety - cedar and blackcurrant in abundance; dust, tobacco and vanilla as backnotes. Pair with basil pesto.

Kitchen Survivor™ Grade: B+

Your notes: _____

Franciscan Magnificat Meritage,   **Pts**
Napa, California 2006   **$43**   **89**

The most elegant Magnificat yet, with minty-dusty, allspice, tobacco and vanilla notes cloaking the dark cherry, plum and berry fruit. Pair with Moroccan-spiced or tandoori chicken to kick up the spice.
Kitchen Survivor™ Grade: B

Your notes: _____

Frog's Leap Cabernet Sauvignon,   **Pts**
Napa, California 2007   **$42**   **91**

I love the brooding, sweet-savory interplay here of sweet dark berry fruit and dusky black olive. The velvet texture and subtlety suggest it will age, too. Pair with pan-roasted quail with red wine-shallot sauce.
Kitchen Survivor™ Grade: B

Your notes: _____

Louis Martini Napa Valley Reserve   **Pts**
Cabernet Sauvignon, Napa, California 2007 $25   **90**

As always, lots of dusty-cedary Napa-ness for the price. The sweet pipe tobacco, blackberry fruit and velvet texture scream for a great blue cheese burger.
Kitchen Survivor™ Grade: B+

Your notes: _____

Robert Mondavi Cabernet Sauvignon,   **Pts**
Napa, California 2007   **$28**   **91**

This Napa blue chip has hit a new quality mark. It is velvety and lush, with rich cassis fruit and a spicy-vanilla-wood char finish. Great with pesto pasta.
Kitchen Survivor™ Grade: C

Your notes: _____

St. Clement Cabernet Sauvignon,   **Pts**
Napa, California 2007   **$35**   **94**

It's hard to find more for the money in Napa Cab. This one's classy and classic, with pencil dust, anise, lively red fruit berries and plums and a warm brick earthiness like French Bordeaux. Great with aged cheeses, a garlicky lamb stew or prime rib.
Kitchen Survivor™ Grade: B+

Your notes: _____

TOP TEN CABERNETS:
NAPA $45 - $100

Caymus Napa Cabernet   **Pts**
Sauvignon, California 2008   **$70**   **90**
Cedary, with blueberry and fudge flavors and satin
tannins. Great with a flatiron steak with sage butter.
Kitchen Survivor™ Grade: B+
Your notes: _____

Beaulieu Vineyard (BV) Tapestry Reserve   **Pts**
Red Blend, Napa, California 2007   **$55**   **91**
A mix of Cab, Merlot, Cabernet Franc, Malbec and
Petit Verdot that layers dusty earth, ripe and dark
berry fruit, smoke and lead pencil, on a suede tex-
ture. Super with sage- and thyme-rubbed pork roast.
Kitchen Survivor™ Grade: B
Your notes: _____

Frank Family Vineyards Cabernet   **Pts**
Sauvignon, Napa, California 2007   **$45**   **96**
"Awestruck" was the vibe at our tasting of this wine,
which stands tall with Napa Cabs at 2-3X the price.
The incredible cinnamon-cedar-vanilla and dense,
3-D blackberry and fig fruit are quintessentially
"Napa Cab." Tee up a great prime steak for this one.
Kitchen Survivor™ Grade: A+
Your notes: _____

Grgich Hills Estate Cabernet Sauvignon,   **Pts**
Napa, California 2006   **$60**   **92**
Grgich eschews the "fruit bomb" model in favor of
chewy dark cherry and tobacco, with an old world-style
mushroomy earthiness. Pair it with garlicky lamb.
Kitchen Survivor™ Grade: A
Your notes: _____

Heitz Cellars Cabernet Sauvignon,   **Pts**
Napa, California 2006   **$45**   **94**
A proud sibling of the famed Martha's Vineyard bot-
tling, and its own special style. The brambly berry
fruit is layered with lusty-savory tar and black olive
notes. A great match for venison with juniper *jus*.
Kitchen Survivor™ Grade: B+
Your notes: _____

Ladera Howell Mountain Cabernet,   **Pts**
Sauvignon, Napa, California 2007 $60   97

One of the best CA Cabs, period, with intense dark fudge, black fig, wet brick and anise, and plush, mouth-coating tannins. Pair with lamb and black olive stew.

Kitchen Survivor™ Grade: B+

Your notes: _____

Mt. Veeder Cabernet Sauvignon,   **Pts**
Napa, California 2007 $50   91

I love the signature style of this wine: dense and chewy, with dark berries, tobacco and cedar, and a long dusty-cocoa finish. Pair it with a smoked brisket to bring out the wine's earthiness. Ages beautifully.

Kitchen Survivor™ Grade: A

Your notes: _____

Beaulieu Vineyard (BV) Georges   **Pts**
de Latour Private Reserve Cabernet $80   95
Sauvignon, Napa, California 2007

Always true to its opulent signature style: tobacco, leather, consomme, with sumptuous dark cherry fruit and a suede texture. Ages beautifully, but it's also delicious young with red wine-braised shortribs.

Kitchen Survivor™ Grade: B

Your notes: _____

Silver Oak Napa Valley   **Pts**
Cabernet Sauvignon, California 2005 $100   94

The extra year in bottle compared to other big Cabs gives this wine extra nuances of brambly gaminess to compliment the succulent dark cherry fruit, and signature coconut, dill and allspice notes. Pair with dark chocolate, or prime rib with caramelized shallots.

Kitchen Survivor™ Grade: B

Your notes: _____

Trefethen Estate Cabernet Sauvignon,   **Pts**
Oak Knoll District, Napa California 2007 $50   94

Such a finessed wine, and true to its signatures of violets, lavender, dark plum, blackberry and sprightly cedar. All those layers make it a stunner with Tuscan steak or soy-marinated duck, but it ages well, too.

Kitchen Survivor™ Grade: B

Your notes: _____

TOP TEN CABERNETS: CALIFORNIA OVER $100

Araujo Cabernet Sauvignon Eisele Vineyard   **Pts**
Napa Valley, California 2007   **$250**   **99**
The Eisele terroir is the source of this wine's power, opulence and purity of black plum and fig fruit and charcoal-y earthiness, framed up by the perfect complement of sweet chocolate fudge oakiness. Pair with a velvety steak and dark chocolate.
Kitchen Survivor™ Grade: B+
Your notes: _____

Beringer Private Reserve Cabernet   **Pts**
Sauvignon, Napa, California 2007   **$116**   **93**
One whiff brings a wave of layers: cedar, olives, tobacco, mint, smoke, cocoa and black cherry. Break out your best cheeses, velvety prime rib, or duck.
Kitchen Survivor™ Grade: B+
Your notes: _____

Dalla Valle Cabernet Sauvignon,   **Pts**
Oakville, Napa, California 2006   **$150**   **94**
Dalla Valle is the elegant lady in the cult Cab realm, dressed (and ready for a duck dinner) in a velvet cloak of anise, wet brick earthiness and dense black cherry.
Kitchen Survivor™ Grade: B+
Your notes: _____

Etude Cabernet Sauvignon, Napa   **Pts**
California 2006   **$125**   **98**
This is a charry-dusty power/finesse phenom. Its pencil dust, mint, succulent cassis and velvet plushness stand with the world's best Cabs.
Kitchen Survivor™ Grade: A+
Your notes: _____

Heitz Cellars Martha's Vineyard Cabernet   **Pts**
Sauvignon, Napa, California 2005   **$150**   **97**
A true Napa classic. California Cab lovers can guess it blind because of the fragrance of mint, cedar and eucalyptus, and the powerful, tarry black cherry and pipe tobacco on the palate. Ages for decades.
Kitchen Survivor™ Grade: A+
Your notes: _____

Ridge Monte Bello, Santa Cruz Mountains, California 2007   **Pts** $145 100

Perfection is this Pandora's box of delights: achingly pure cassis and dark cherry fruit, tree bark and smoke earthiness, chocolate-dipped espresso and vanilla beans, carried to your palate on a velvet cushion.

Kitchen Survivor™ Grade: B+

Your notes: _____

Robert Mondavi Cabernet Sauvignon Reserve, Napa, California 2007   **Pts** $135 96

A Napa blue chip that's both powerful and elegant, with layers of briary tobacco, dark cherry, bitter chocolate and cassis notes. Ages beautifully for decades.

Kitchen Survivor™ Grade: B+

Your notes: _____

Shafer Hillside Select Cabernet Sauvignon, Stags Leap District, Napa, California 2006   **Pts** $215 96

An opulent expression of Stags Leap District terroir - sassafras, warm brick, rosemary and anise. Rich fig and cherry, chocolate and sweet spices echo into the smoky finish. One for the cellar, or a fine steak.

Kitchen Survivor™ Grade: B+

Your notes: _____

Staglin Family Estate Cabernet Sauvignon, Napa Valley, California 2007   **Pts** $175 100

Luxuriance *and* dusty terroir equals perfection. The layers of briary blackberry and fig, cacao, vanilla bean, charcoal and lavender command your attention, so keep the food subtle - rare duck breast or prime steak.

Kitchen Survivor™ Grade: A+

Your notes: _____

Stag's Leap Cask 23 Cabernet Sauvignon, Stags Leap District, Napa, California 2007   **Pts** $195 99

The wine that won the famous Paris tasting in 1976 and put Napa Cab on the map remains a rockstar of terroir. It is fragrant with violets, sweet tarragon, cedar and anise, and juicy with dark cherry and singed plum fruit, plus whiffs of savory herbs in the finish. Fabulous with rosemary-rubbed rack of lamb.

Kitchen Survivor™ Grade: A+

Your notes: _____

TOP TEN FRENCH RED BORDEAUX UNDER $50

		Pts
Chateau d'Angludet, Margaux, Bordeaux, France 2007	**$28**	**93**

One of the best 2007s with a keepin'-it-real price. Vivid dark cherry fruit with juicy acidity and sleek, cedary-spicy tannins. A great way to taste Medoc terroir, and an affordable ager. Pair with a smoky duck and bean stew.

Kitchen Survivor™ Grade: B+

Your notes: _____

		Pts
Chateau Beaumont, Haut-Medoc, Bordeaux, France 2007	**$25**	**91**

Medoc style *par excellence*: pencil dust, cedar, leafy earthiness, blackcurrant fruit and a mocha finish. I chose this for Delta to please the winegeeks, but newbies will love it, too. Pairs with all but the lightest fish dishes, and be sure to keep a splash in your glass for the cheese course!

Kitchen Survivor™ Grade: B+

Your notes: _____

		Pts
Chateau Chasse-Spleen, Moulis-en-Medoc, Bordeaux France 2007	**$35**	**91**

Terrific concentration and length, with charred meat and caramelized shallot notes underpinning the structured blackcurrant fruit. Pair with a rich beef stew.

Kitchen Survivor™ Grade: B+

Your notes: _____

		Pts
Chateau Cantemerle, Haut-Medoc, Bordeaux France 2007	**$31**	**89**

The rich core of plum fruit is wrapped in savory layers of green peppercorn and coriander on a sleek frame. Pair with a lusty rabbit and black olive stew. Mmm!

Kitchen Survivor™ Grade: B+

Your notes: _____

		Pts
Chateau de Pez, Saint-Estephe, Bordeaux, France 2007	**$42**	**95**

Worth the trade-up - this beat many famous chateaus in my tastings. The core is ripe dark cherry fruit, wrapped in layers of cedar spice, mocha and vanilla. Pair with red

wine-braised shortribs or mild cheeses such as Brebis.
Kitchen Survivor™ Grade: A+
Your notes: _____

Chateau Greysac Medoc, Bordeaux, France 2007
$22   **Pts 88**

Elegant! Lovely cassis, violets and espresso scents plus a round and plummy mid-palate. It all adds up to a sleek and balanced partner for grilled quail and mushrooms.
Kitchen Survivor™ Grade: B
Your notes: _____

Chateau Marquis de Terme, Margaux, France 2007
$45   **Pts 91**

Lavished with toasty-vanilla oak in a more new world style, with classic sweet cassis fruit, pencil dust and smoke notes that pair perfectly with charred lamb chops, grilled steak with wine sauce, or fine cheeses.
Kitchen Survivor™ Grade: B+
Your notes: _____

Chateau Ormes de Pez, Saint-Estephe, Bordeaux, France 2007
$31   **Pts 94**

The exotic fig, chocolate and vanilla notes are almost flamboyant, but the wine's fabulous structure and dusty-earthy finish keep it classic. Pair with a cheesy, buttery, mushroomy pasta to let the fruit shine.
Kitchen Survivor™ Grade: B+
Your notes: _____

Chateau Poujeaux, Moulis-en-Medoc, Bordeaux, France 2007
$29   **Pts 90**

Fragrant camphor, cedar and dark plums add intrigue to the meal-in-a-glass flavors of beef stock and caramelized shallots with dark cherry. Pot roast, anyone?
Kitchen Survivor™ Grade: B+
Your notes: _____

Chateau du Tertre, Margaux, Bordeaux, France 2007
$35   **Pts 92**

Hello, barnyard!...and smoke, mint, sassafras, tree bark, worn leather; the lusty layers are a Francophile's dream. Pair with game, pates and earthy cheeses.
Kitchen Survivor™ Grade: B+
Your notes: _____

TOP TEN FRENCH RED BORDEAUX OVER $50

Chateau Angelus, Saint-Emilion, Bordeaux, France 2007   **Pts**
     $180   **96**

"Worth the money if you have it" is the best way to put it, because this wine rocks. The lavish sweet oak is matched by equally intense cherry and chocolate. Not "typical" Bordeaux, but great. Pair with a rich, mild cheese and let the wine own the spotlight.
Kitchen Survivor™ Grade: B
Your notes: _____

Chateau Beychevelle, Saint-Julien, Bordeaux, France 2007   **Pts**
     $54   **91**

Fragrant violets and cassis on the nose, dense plum, cedar and dustiness on the palate and finish. The grippy tannins soften with air, and the right food partner. Try slow-cooker pot roast or wine-braised duck.
Kitchen Survivor™ Grade: B+
Your notes: _____

Chateau Canon, Saint-Emilion, Bordeaux, France 2007   **Pts**
     $65   **93**

A sleek and classic expression of Saint-Emilion terroir with a violet perfume, plum and cassis fruit, great structure and finesse. Pair with a subtle roast duck.
Kitchen Survivor™ Grade: B+
Your notes: _____

Chateau Clinet, Pomerol, Bordeaux, France 2007   **Pts**
     $60   **92**

SO Bordeaux: toasty espresso and roast beefy scent and firm, dusty tannins cloaking the rich plum fruit. Needs aging and a rich table-mate such as prime rib.
Kitchen Survivor™ Grade: A+
Your notes: _____

Chateau Gazin, Pomerol, Bordeaux, France 2007   **Pts**
     $54   **91**

The stylistic opposite of my other Pomerol pick, this is all suppleness and silky plum fruit, with the classic mocha/espresso terroir. Pair with a rich coq au vin.
Kitchen Survivor™ Grade: B+
Your notes: _____

Chateau Giscours, Margaux,   **Pts**
Bordeaux, France 2007 $60   90

The savory pepper and beef stock scent sets you up for a gamy savoriness of caramelized shallots and bacon-wrapped figs on the palate. The medium body, tug of tannin and earthy finish makes that a great match!

Kitchen Survivor™ Grade: B+

Your notes: _____

Chateau Lascombes, Margaux,   **Pts**
Bordeaux, France 2007 $60   93

A Tiramisu coffee-sweetness sets you up for a dense mouthful of dark cassis, lead pencil and cedar, and looong finish. Pair with Moroccan-spiced lamb stew.

Kitchen Survivor™ Grade: A+

Your notes: _____

Chateau Leoville-Poyferre, Saint-Julien,   **Pts**
Bordeaux, France 2007 $63   91

Elegant, but with nice concentration and structure to the layered dark cherry and cedar spice. The smoky, long finish makes it a great match for a smoked beef filet or rack of pork, or pasta with morel mushrooms.

Kitchen Survivor™ Grade: B

Your notes: _____

Chateau Lynch-Bages, Pauillac,   **Pts**
Bordeaux, France 2007 $77   96

Cedar-a-go-go and cassis scent+dark cherries and beef-in-a-glass=classic Lynch-Bages. The flavor density and structure will carry it for 15+ years in the cellar. Serve with rosemary- and wine- braised lamb.

Kitchen Survivor™ Grade: B+

Your notes: _____

Clos Fourtet, Saint-Emilion,   **Pts**
Bordeaux, France 2007 $50   93

My sentimental favorite (the first really old bottle I ever tried) is still a quality star. Coffee, mocha and sweet vanilla scents unfold to sweet dark cherry fruit on the palate and tightly-wound spicy tannins to carry it for the long haul. Pair with a truffly, cheesy pasta.

Kitchen Survivor™ Grade: A+

Your notes: _____

Spanish Reds

Category Profile: Like other classic European wines, it's the place—called a Denominación de Origen (DO)—rather than the grape on a Spanish wine label, in most cases. Spain's signature red grape, used in both the Rioja (*ree-OH-huh*) and the Ribera del Duero (*ree-BEAR-uh dell DWAIR-oh*) DOs, is called Tempranillo (*temp-rah-NEE-oh*). Depending on quality level, the style of Rioja ranges from easy drinking and spicy to seriously rich, leathery/toffee. Ribera del Duero is generally big and tannic. The other Spanish reds here are from Priorat (*pre-oh-RAHT*), known for strong, inky-dark cellar candidates (usually made from Tempranillo, Cabernet, and/or Grenache). Though not represented in my Top Ten, Penedes (*pen-eh-DESS*), which is better known for Cava sparkling wines, is also an outstanding source of values in every style and color.

Serve: Cool room temperature; as a rule Spanish reds are exemplary food wines, but basic reds from Penedes and Rioja (with the word *Cosecha* or *Crianza* on the label), and emerging regions like Navarra, Toro, and Somontano, are good "anytime" wines and tasty on their own.

When: If you dine out often in wine-focused restaurants, Spanish reds are *the* red wine category for world-class drinking that's also affordable.

With: The classic matches are pork and lamb, either roasted or grilled; also amazing with slow-roasted chicken or turkey and hams, sausages, and other cured meats. Finally, try a Spanish Ribera del Duero, Priorat, or Rioja Reserva or Gran Reserva with good-quality cheese. (Spanish Manchego is wonderful and available in supermarkets.)

In: The One™ glass for red wines, or a larger-bowled red wine stem.

Almost Top Ten Spanish Reds:

These wines are also well worth checking out.

Marques de Caceres Rioja Crianza
Comenge Ribera del Duero
Val Llach Priorat
Emilio Moro Ribera del Duero
Valduero Ribera del Duero
Torres Gran Coronas Black Label

"Worth the splurge" Spanish Reds:

Marques de Grinon
Clos Mogador
Vega Sicilia Valbuena

TOP TEN SPANISH REDS: $25 OR LESS

Abadia Retuerta Rivola,   **Pts**
Sardon de Duero, Spain 2008   **$14**   **89**

This 60/40 Tempranillo/Cab blend is all juicy red plums, mint, pepper and sweet balsamic - a love letter to savory dishes like barbecue or teriyaki.

Kitchen Survivor™ Grade: B

Your notes: _____

Abadia Retuerta Seleccion Especial,   **Pts**
Sardon de Duero, Spain 2007   **$20**   **91**

This Tempranillo with a touch of Merlot and Cab is inky and exotic, with cherry kirsch, bitter chocolate and allspice plus a savory black olive note. More layers will unfold with age. In the meantime, pair with a rich Moroccan-spiced lamb tagine or olive tapenade.

Kitchen Survivor™ Grade: A+

Your notes: _____

Bodegas O. Fournier Urban Ribera del   **Pts**
Duero Roble, Spain 2007   **$14**   **90**

A heady mouthful for the money, with dense fig and balsamic flavors and sweet coriander spice. A magic match for cheeses, rustic mushroom dishes and lamb.

Kitchen Survivor™ Grade: B+

Your notes: _____

Bordon Rioja Gran Reserva,   **Pts**
Spain 2001   **$24**   **92**

It's exciting to have a bottle-aged pick like this for Delta because the bewitching leather, mushrooms, meat stock, tobacco, dark spiced figs and satin texture just aren't your typical airline wine. Pair with poultry, beef and of course, the cheese course!

Kitchen Survivor™ Grade: B+

Your notes: _____

Borsao Tinto Garnacha/Tempranillo,   **Pts**
Campo de Borja, Spain 2009   **$8**   **88**

The juicy candied cherry fruit and nice spice of this wine let you "yum out" on the cheap. Pair with chili, burritos, blackened chicken or barbecue.

Kitchen Survivor™ Grade: B+

Your notes: _____

El Coto de Imaz Rioja Reserva, Spain 2004

$15   **Pts 91**

Gorgeous and classically styled with heady scents and flavors of sweet brandied cherries, cinnamon, toffee and a hint of leather. The depth on the palate and wonderful structure ensure this wine will evolve beautifully for another 10 years. Fabulous with Manchego cheese, lamb chops, and serrano ham.

Kitchen Survivor™ Grade: B+

Your notes: _____

Faustino V Rioja Reserva, Rioja, Spain 2004

$20   **Pts 94**

More character than many Riojas at twice the price: leather toffee, pepper and satin-smoothness with sweet cherries on the palate. Pair with lamb chops.

Kitchen Survivor™ Grade: B+

Your notes: _____

Federico Tinto Ribera del Duero, Spain 2007

$17   **Pts 90**

Traditional-style Ribera with lots of leather, grip and cured meat complexity gracing the dark plum and pepper spice. A great match with sausage pizza.

Kitchen Survivor™ Grade: B+

Your notes: _____

Mibal Ribera del Duero, Spain 2006

$14   **Pts 89**

A super deal for the complexity and yum factor: sweet roasted beet earthiness, charcoal and wild dark berries. Perfect for savory-sweet barbecued ribs.

Kitchen Survivor™ Grade: B+

Your notes: _____

Palacios Remondo La Montesa Rioja Crianza, Spain 2007

$20   **Pts 89**

A Garnacha-dominated blend with Tempranillo, Mazuelo and Graciano. The juicy red fruit and cumin spice make it a great match for pork chile verde.

Kitchen Survivor™ Grade: C

Your notes: _____

TOP TEN SPANISH REDS:
ABOVE $25

Aalto Ribera del Duero,   **Pts**
Spain 2007   **$54**   **92**

Pen ink, blueberries and bitter chocolate and fragrant vanilla bean make this an exotic and complex mouthful. Pair with a creamy, cheesy mushroom risotto.

Kitchen Survivor™ Grade: A+

Your notes: _____

Baron de Ley Rioja Gran Reserva,   **Pts**
Spain 1998   **$38**   **95**

The magic of Rioja Gran Reserva is you can find these bottle-aged beauties for affordable prices. This one is all coconut-toffee, mushroom consomme and silk on the palate. Pair it with a silky grilled salmon and wild mushrooms - unforgettable!

Kitchen Survivor™ Grade: B+

Your notes: _____

Bohorquez Ribera del Duero   **Pts**
Spain 2005   **$34**   **90**

The extra time in bottle layers ink, charred wood and bitter chocolate notes atop the briary, pepper berry flavors. Pair with olive tapenade or jerk-spiced pork.

Kitchen Survivor™ Grade: B

Your notes: _____

La Rioja Alta Vina Ardanza Reserva,   **Pts**
Spain 2000   **$35**   **92**

Textbook traditional Rioja Reserva: tangy cranberry, sweet caramel, leather and caramelized onion notes that make it a stunning match with roast game.

Kitchen Survivor™ Grade: B

Your notes: _____

Marques de Murrieta Castillo Ygay Rioja,   **Pts**
Gran Reserva Especial, Spain 2001   **$54**   **96**

Although there's loads of browned butter, balsamic, black pepper and olive earthiness, the wine's taut acidity and dense cherries jubilee fruit will carry it for decades with grace. Pair with butter and sage pasta.

Kitchen Survivor™ Grade: A+

Your notes: _____

Marques de Riscal Rioja Gran
Reserva, Spain 2000 $35   Pts
                                              90
Traditional Rioja at its best: date and dried figs;
leather, chewy tannins; and great spice, with a long
buttery-coconut finish. A great match for sauteed
mushrooms with garlic, or grilled lamb chops.
Kitchen Survivor™ Grade: B+

Your notes: _____

Muga (*MOO-guh*) Rioja Reserva,
Spain 2006 $26   Pts
                                              90
"Muga" is Spanish for world-class. The dense mince-
meat, chewy dried cherry and brown spice notes, and
suede-smooth tannins are the house style signature.
Pair with manchego cheese, good bread and olive oil.
Kitchen Survivor™ Grade: A+

Your notes: _____

Pesquera (*pess-CARE-uh*) Crianza, Ribera
del Duero, Spain 2006 $35   Pts
                                              91
A big and brooding wine. The scents of violets, tar
and dark berries, and palate of dense tannins and
plum liqueur, will harmonize with cellaring. When
young, pair with roast game or rich cheeses.
Kitchen Survivor™ Grade: B+

Your notes: _____

R. Lopez de Heredia Vina Bosconia Rioja
Reserva, Spain 2001 $36   Pts
                                              94
A young wine for Lopez de Heredia, the classic tradi-
tionalist: aged forever yet seemingly ageless. Start
with this silky, mushroomy, leathery classic and a
great cheese - but try 'em all, white and rose, too.
Kitchen Survivor™ Grade: B+

Your notes: _____

Teofilo Reyes Ribera del Duero,
Spain 2004 $63   Pts
                                              94
Warm brick and wet metal, sassafras, sweet black
plums and peppered figs - and that's before the wine
has been cellared, which is its true calling. Leather,
truffle, brown spices and tobacco emerge with bottle
age. Pair with earthy dishes such as mushroom ravioli
or a duck and sausage cassoulet.
Kitchen Survivor™ Grade: A+

Your notes: _____

Uncommon Red Grapes & Blends

Category Profile: As with the whites, this isn't a cohesive category but rather a spot to put worthy, interesting reds that don't neatly fit a grape or region category—namely, proprietary blends, and uncommon varietals.

Proprietary Blends—These may be tasty, inexpensive blends or ambitious signature blends at luxury prices.

Uncommon Varietals—These are quite exciting. I introduced Malbec and Carmenere in the Merlot section, because I think they are distinctive and delicious alternatives for Merlot lovers. Although the names and even the style (bold and a little peppery) are similar, Petite Sirah and Syrah (Shiraz) are not the same grape. Gamay also comes in here in its classical form - French Beaujolais.

Serve: Cool room temperature, or even slightly chilled.

When: Anytime you need an interesting, value-priced red.

With: Anything from snacks to fine meals. These are very food-friendly!

In: The One™ glass for red wines, an all-purpose wineglass or a larger-bowled wineglass.

GAMAY & BEAUJOLAIS: Beaujolais (*bow-jhoe-LAY*) Nouveau, the new wine of the vintage that each year is shipped from France on the third Thursday in November (just in time for Thanksgiving), dominates sales in this category. You can have fun with nouveau, but don't skip the real stuff—particularly Beaujolais-Villages (*vill-AHJH*) and Beaujolais Cru (named for the town where it is grown, for example, Morgon, Brouilly, and Moulin-à-Vent). These Beaujolais categories are a wine world rarity, in that they offer real character at a low price. The signature style of Beaujolais is a juicy, grapey fruit flavor and succulent texture with, in the crus, an added layer of earthy spiciness. That makes it a natural, easy food partner with everything from the Thanksgiving spread to the simplest of sandwich meals, to brunch, lunch, and beyond. All red Beaujolais is made from the Gamay grape. Georges Duboeuf, the "King of Beaujolais" (by far the most famous and largest producer) calls 2009 the "vintage of a lifetime" and I agree, so don't miss it!

TOP TEN UNCOMMON REDS

Argento Malbec   **Pts**
Mendoza, Argentina 2008   **$9**   **89**

So much more blueberries-and-chocolate character than most under-$10 Malbecs. This one's juicy and velvety, and a great match for grilled cheeseburgers.
Kitchen Survivor™ Grade: C

Your notes: _____

Casa Lapostolle Carmenere Cuvee,   **Pts**
Alexandre, Colchagua, Chile 2009   **$14**   **92**

Suede texture, black cherries, cumin, beef tartare and game notes - this is a serious wine for a steal price. Pair with funky cheeses, chili, dark chocolate. Yum!
Kitchen Survivor™ Grade: B

Your notes: _____

Duboeuf (Georges) Beaujolais-   **Pts**
Villages, France 2009   **$12**   **90**

Mr. Duboeuf calls 2009 the "vintage of a lifetime" meaning he's never seen better quality. I agree! This wine has fantastic depth of plum fruit and a dried-leaf earthiness that makes it a great partner with roast chicken, meatloaf, pates and slow-cooked stews.
Kitchen Survivor™ Grade: B

Your notes: _____

Bogle Petite Sirah,   **Pts**
California 2008   **$12**   **88**

A black pepper and berries mouthful that's always an awesome value, and a great match for barbecue.
Kitchen Survivor™ Grade: B

Your notes: _____

Catena Alta Malbec, Mendoza,   **Pts**
Argentina 2007   **$40**   **92**

Powerful, layered, complex. The blackberry fruit, velvet tannins, sweet vanilla bean and five-spice notes are graced with a wet slate minerality in the finish. Pair with a simple truffled pasta or osso buco.
Kitchen Survivor™ Grade: B

Your notes: _____

Concannon 'The Conservancy' Petite   **Pts**
Sirah, Livermore 2007   **$12**   **89**

This is Concannon's signature grape for a reason - it's delish! The full-blooded meaty, peppery, wild berry notes beg for barbecued ribs or a bowl of chili.

Kitchen Survivor™ Grade: B+

Your notes: _____

Lang & Reed Cabernet Franc '214',   **Pts**
Napa 2007   **$40**   **92**

How I adore the wild raspberry, violets, sweet tarragon and crushed mint layers of this wine. The mid-palate succulence is just lipsmacking. Pair with dark chocolate or herb-crusted Brin d'Amour cheese. Ooh.

Kitchen Survivor™ Grade: B

Your notes: _____

Miner Family Sangiovese Gibson Ranch,   **Pts**
Mendocino, California 2007   **$20**   **91**

A gulper whose strawberry-rhubarb jam, white pepper and blood orange flavors just sing out of the glass, and I think "food, glorious food" is the tune--any questions?

Kitchen Survivor™ Grade: B+

Your notes: _____

Salentein Malbec Reserve,   **Pts**
Argentina 2007   **$20**   **90**

Richer, more sophisticated and more complex than most Argentinian Malbecs. Dark boysenberry fruit with varietally-typical notes of pen ink, roast beef and leather underneath the soft vanilla and spice. A real attention-getter. Pair with a great steak.

Kitchen Survivor™ Grade: B+

Your notes: _____

Veramonte Primus,   **Pts**
Chile 2007   **$17**   **90**

This pioneer Carmenere blend is always a favorite of mine for its wild dark berries, licorice, and savory fennel seed and cumin complexity. Pair with sausage pizza, chicken mole poblano or pork chile verde.

Kitchen Survivor™ Grade: B

Your notes: _____

Syrah/Shiraz &
Other Rhone-Style Reds

Category Profile: The varietal Shiraz, Australia's signature red, is so hot that many pros say it has unseated Merlot as consumers' go-to grape. Popularity has its price for Shiraz lovers, though, because many of the biggest brands have begun to taste like generic red wine rather than the spunky-spicy Shiraz with which we fell in love. I've focused on brands that have stayed true to the Shiraz varietal character. The same grape, under the French spelling *Syrah,* also forms the backbone for France's revered Rhone Valley reds with centuries-old reputations. These include Cotes-du-Rhone (*coat-duh-ROAN*), Cote-Rotie (*ro-TEE*), Hermitage (*uhr-muh-TAHJ*), and Chateauneuf-du-Pape (*shah-toe-NUFF-duh-POP*), and their satellite appellations Crozes-Hermitage, St. Joseph and . Like basic Shiraz, Cotes-du-Rhone, with its lovely spicy fruit character, is a value star. The latter three are true French classics and, in my view, currently lead that elite group in quality for the money. They are full-bodied, powerful, peppery, earthy, concentrated, and oak aged. Finally, most major American wineries, and many smaller players, are bottling California or Washington State versions, often labeled with the Aussie spelling *Shiraz* rather than the French *Syrah.*

Serve: Cool room temperature; aeration enhances the aroma and flavor.

When: Basic Syrah/Shiraz and Cotes-du-Rhone are great everyday drinking wines; in restaurants, these are great go-to categories for relative value.

With: Grilled, barbecued, or roasted anything (including fish and vegetables); outstanding with steaks, fine cheeses, and other dishes that call for a full red wine; I also love these styles with traditional Thanksgiving fare.

In: The One™ glass for red wines, an all-purpose wineglass or a larger-bowled wineglass.

Almost Top Ten Pinot Syrah/Shiraz & Rhone-Style Reds:

These wines are also well worth checking out.

Jaboulet Crozes-Hermitage Les Jalets
Clape Cornas
Duboeuf Cotes du Rhone
Perrin Cotes du Rhone Reserve
Jaboulet Cote-Rotie Les Jumelles
Geoff Merrill

"Worth the splurge" Syrah/Shiraz & Rhone-Style:

Chateau de Beaucastel Chateauneuf-du-Pape
Penfolds Grange
Clarendon Hills
Jim Barry
Mt. Langhi Ghiran

TOP TEN SYRAH/SHIRAZ: NEW WORLD UNDER $20

Alice White Shiraz,   **Pts**
Australia 2008   **$6**   **87**

This wine still delivers the wild raspberry fruit and spice that first lured us to budget Aussie Shiraz. Bring on the BBQ and, at this price, you can afford to host the block party!

Kitchen Survivor™ Grade: C

Your notes: _____

D'Arenberg The Footbolt Shiraz,   **Pts**
Australia 2008   **$15**   **89**

I love the softness and gamy-spicy-plummy richness of this wine, a yummy match for BBQ or pizza.

Kitchen Survivor™ Grade: B

Your notes: _____

Jacob's Creek Reserve Shiraz,   **Pts**
Australia 2007   **$11**   **90**

Eucalyptus, mint and black peppery fig scents and flavors - that's a lot of character for a budget bottle. Great with BBQ, teriyaki, or blackened chicken.

Kitchen Survivor™ Grade: C

Your notes: _____

Jacob's Creek Shiraz/Cabernet   **Pts**
Sauvignon, Australia 2007   **$8**   **89**

This wine offers great taste and great value, with lush raspberry and eucalyptus notes and a plush texture.

Kitchen Survivor™ Grade: B

Your notes: _____

Morgan Syrah, Monterey,   **Pts**
California 2008   **$18**   **90**

Yay for varietal character! That means pepper, wild berry fruit, lavender and a smoky funkiness that's just awesome. Bring on the Texas-style smoky beef BBQ.

Kitchen Survivor™ Grade: B

Your notes: _____

Penfolds Koonunga Hill Shiraz   Pts
Cabernet, Australia 2008 $11   88

Plummy-spicy scents and flavors, and the dollop of Cab in the blend gives a nice grip that stands up to hearty slow-cooker stews and pot roasts.
Kitchen Survivor™ *Grade: C*

Your notes: _____

Qupe Central Coast Syrah,   Pts
California 2008 $17   93

The best US Syrah for the money, to be sure. It's all-there: white pepper, lavender, coriander and allspice, languorous sweet raspberry and strawberry fruit, pomegranate-tangy herbaceousness. Just add ratatouille, fennel sausage, tapenade and goat cheese.
Kitchen Survivor™ *Grade: B+*

Your notes: _____

Rosemount Diamond Label Shiraz-   Pts
Cabernet, South Eastern Australia 2008 $10   89

My favorite of the Diamond Label series - a juicy raspberry-spice yum-bomb that's great "house red" material and fills the bill with everyday meals: take-out, pizza, pasta, panini, burgers, you name it.
Kitchen Survivor™ *Grade: C*

Your notes: _____

Wente Syrah, Livermore,   Pts
California 2008 $12   89

Syrah character at a budget price-yay! The wild berry and plum fruit with a whiff of pepper spice are just the ticket for sausage pizza or jerk-spiced chicken.
Kitchen Survivor™ *Grade: C*

Your notes: _____

Wolf-Blass Yellow Label Shiraz,   Pts
South Eastern Australia 2008 $9   89

More Aussie Shiraz-ness for the money than 95% of the budget competition. The juicy mid-palate of black pepper-spiced red and black fruits with a whisper of licorice makes it a yummy match for spicy sushi or dry-rubbed barbecued ribs.
Kitchen Survivor™ *Grade: B*

Your notes: _____

TOP TEN SYRAH/SHIRAZ: NEW WORLD ABOVE $20

Cape Mentelle Shiraz, Australia 2006   **Pts** $30   93

A FAVE wine that screams terroir, with alluring eucalyptus, mint wild raspberry and sweet herb notes, and a luxuriant texture. Pair with lamb stew with olives or turkey with sage stuffing to showcase the layers.
Kitchen Survivor™ Grade: A+
Your notes: _____

Fleming-Jenkins Syrah, Santa Cruz 2007   **Pts** $37   91

A real winner among US Syrahs for its true varietal expression of black pepper, leather and wild berries, and impeccable balance. A brilliant match for pork chile verde or goat cheese and fennel sausage pizza.
Kitchen Survivor™ Grade: B
Your notes: _____

Kendall-Jackson Highland Estates Alisos, Hills Syrah, Santa Barbara, CA 2006   **Pts** $35   94

Gorgeous old world-style Syrah terroir (black olive, black pepper, tar and lavender), with new world lush dark fig fruit. Pair with steak tartare or sage pasta.
Kitchen Survivor™ Grade: A+
Your notes: _____

Lynmar Syrah, Russian River Valley, California 2007   **Pts** $36   92

Pure allure: lush raspberry-rhubarb fruit, plus old leather, smoke, dusty pepper and cured meat scents. Pair with olive tapenade and goat cheese crostini.
Kitchen Survivor™ Grade: B+
Your notes: _____

Morgan Double "L" Syrah, Santa Lucia Highlands, Monterey, California 2007   **Pts** $40   93

LOVE the cardamom, black pepper and smoky tea notes that add intrigue to the ripe raspberry and fig fruit. Pair with ricotta and fresh herb ravioli.
Kitchen Survivor™ Grade: B+
Your notes: _____

Penfolds Kalimna Shiraz Bin 28,   **Pts**
South Australia 2007   **$25**   **91**

A spiced Christmas fruitcake in a glass. Mint, chocolate, sweet coconut and black olive notes emerge with aeration and the right food partner. Five-spice duck or Asian-style crisp-skinned pork belly would be perfect.
Kitchen Survivor™ Grade: B
Your notes: _____

Penfolds St. Henri Shiraz, South   **Pts**
Australia 2006   **$60**   **95**

Decades-old bottles are wonders to behold, but it already shows amazing complexity in youth: savory herbs, leather, green olives, dried spices, meat stock, sassafras. A simple smoked meat or bird with earthy braised root vegetables will showcase all the layers.
Kitchen Survivor™ Grade: A+
Your notes: _____

Rosemount Show Reserve McLaren Vale
GSM (Grenache-Shiraz-Mourvedre),   **Pts**
Australia 2006   **$24**   **90**

Grenache and Mourvedre contribute a gamy duck stock note to the classic raspberry and sweet spices in this silky wine. Pairing with a fig-stuffed pork loin or five-spice duck will bring out all the flavors.
Kitchen Survivor™ Grade: B
Your notes: _____

Tablas Creek Cotes de Tablas red blend,   **Pts**
Paso Robles, California 2008   **$25**   **91**

Blending Rhone grapes in the Chateauneuf-du-Pape style (Grenache, Syrah, Counoise, Mourvedre) makes this a juicy mouthful, with sweet and tangy red fruits, licorice, mint and blood orange layers from nose to finish. A yummy match for pasta Bolognese.
Kitchen Survivor™ Grade: A+
Your notes: _____

Zaca Mesa Syrah,   **Pts**
Santa Ynez, California 2007   **$23**   **90**

It's simple math: black pepper, smoke, tea and black olives, plus sumptuous blackberry fruit, equals a great deal for the price. Splurge on the steak instead!
Kitchen Survivor™ Grade: B+
Your notes: _____

TOP TEN FRENCH SYRAH/ RHONE REDS

Alain Graillot Crozes-Hermitage **Pts**
Rhone, France 2007 $34 92

Terroir a-go-go, expressed as pomegranate-cured, black pepper-sprinkled bacon. Pair with garlicky leg of lamb or juniper-scented roasted venison.
Kitchen Survivor™ Grade: A+

Your notes: _____

Chapoutier Cotes-du-Rhone 'Belleruche' **Pts**
Rhone, France 2008 $11 89

This wine's alluring white pepper, red currant and blood orange flavors are delicious with bouillabaisse or fish grilled whole with herbs and olive oil.
Kitchen Survivor™ Grade: B

Your notes: _____

Chapoutier Hermitage Monier de la **Pts**
Sizeranne, Rhone, France 2007 $90 91

Composted dark cherries sprinkled with black pepper, tobacco and smoke are the essence of this chewy, powerful wine for the cellar. Pair it with braised shortribs.
Kitchen Survivor™ Grade: A+

Your notes: _____

Coudoulet de Beaucastel Cotes-du- **Pts**
Rhone, Rhone, France 2008 $25 90

Like a "baby" Chateauneuf-du-Pape, this has layers of red plum and currant fruit with white pepper, coriander and fennel spice notes that make it a great match for grilled Italian sausages or sage-rubbed grilled pork.
Kitchen Survivor™ Grade: B

Your notes: _____

Domaine du Vieux Telegraphe Chateauneuf- **Pts**
du-Pape, Rhone, France 2007 $70 94

The power of this wine comes from its concentration and complexity: leather, tobacco, sassafras and deep red cherry fruit, from nose to finish. It's really meant for the cellar but pairing it with rabbit or chicken stewed with black olives, tomatoes and herbs will bring out the spice, tobacco and leather terroir beautifully.
Kitchen Survivor™ Grade: A+

Your notes: _____

Domaine Grand Veneur Chateauneuf-   **Pts**
du-Pape, Rhone, France 2007   **$45**   **92**

Track this one down because the complexity for the
money is stellar: sweet and savory herbs, pomegranate
and strawberry fruit, snappy white pepper and caraway
notes, all in perfect harmony. Goat cheese pizza and
tomato and caper-sauced grilled tuna are great matches.
Kitchen Survivor™ Grade: B+

Your notes: _____

E & M Guigal Cote-Rotie Brune et   **Pts**
Blonde, Rhone, France 2007   **$57**   **94**

You can't get more FAVE than this Cote-Rotie, with
its layers of charcoal, smoke, black olive, pepper and
lavender, plush blackberry fruit, grippy-spicy tannins
and a long, pomegranate-floral finish. It will age 20
years but if you can't wait, pair with braised lamb.
Kitchen Survivor™ Grade: A+

Your notes: _____

E & M Guigal Cotes du Rhone   **Pts**
Rhone, France 2007   **$12**   **89**

A perennial value with loads of character and strawberry-rhubarb and fennel-pepper yumminess. Perfect
with herbed goat cheese or spicy grilled sausages.
Kitchen Survivor™ Grade: A

Your notes: _____

Jaboulet Cotes-du-Rhone Parallele 45   **Pts**
Rhone, France 2008   **$14**   **89**

Potpourri, smoke and black pepper scents, red plum
and licorice flavors, lots of character for the money!
Great with tapenade, paella or pasta Bolognese.
Kitchen Survivor™ Grade: B+

Your notes: _____

La Vieille Ferme Cotes-du-Ventoux   **Pts**
Rhone, France 2008   **$9**   **88**

Silky raspberry, rhubarb and spices make this a value
classic and one of the most "foodie" everyday wines
around. Pair with pizza, panini, pasta, barbecue,
meatloaf...pretty much anything!
Kitchen Survivor™ Grade: B

Your notes: _____

Red Zinfandel

Category Profile: *Groupie* is the apt moniker for devotees of this California specialty, which ranges in style from medium-bodied, with bright and juicy raspberry flavors, to lush, full-bodied, and high in alcohol with intense blueberry, licorice, and even chocolate scents and flavors. Many of the best vineyards have old vines that produce some amazingly intense, complex wines. Zins usually are oaky—a little or a lot, depending on the intensity of the grapes used. The grape intensity is a function of the vineyard—its age and its location. California's most famous red Zinfandel areas are Sonoma (especially the Dry Creek Valley subdistrict), Napa, Amador, and the Sierra foothills. Lodi, in California's Central Valley, is also a good source.

Serve: Room temperature; aeration enhances the aroma and flavor.

When: Value Zinfandels are excellent for everyday drinking; good restaurant lists usually have a selection worth exploring across the price spectrum.

With: Burgers, pizza, lamb (especially with Indian or Moroccan spices), and quality cheeses are favorites—even dark chocolate!

In: The One™ glass for red wines, or a larger-bowled red wine stem.

Almost Top Ten Zinfandel:

These wines are also well worth checking out.

Inspiration
Tres Sabores
Deloach
Gnarly Head
Renwood
Rafanelli
Rosenblum

"Worth the splurge" Zinfandels:

Martinelli Jackass Vineyard
Williams-Selyem
Ravenswood Teldeschi

TOP TEN RED ZINFANDELS

7 Deadly Zins Zinfandel, Lodi,   **Pts**
California 2008   **$9**   **87**

Hugely popular and why not? It's fun and gulpable with plenty of soft blackberry, spice and sweet balsamic flavors. Barbecue, anyone?

Kitchen Survivor™ Grade: C

Your notes: _____

Bogle Old Vines Zinfandel,   **Pts**
California 2008   **$11**   **87**

Nice Zin character - blackberry, molasses and black pepper - for a nice price. Pair with ribs or burgers.

Kitchen Survivor™ Grade: C

Your notes: _____

Frank Family Zinfandel, Napa Valley,   **Pts**
California 2008   **$35**   **94**

Pepper-sprinkled, sun-warmed berries with a hint of smoke and tar. This is a "big" Zin that tastes delish on its own, yet has the FAVE balance to share the table with game birds, grilled meats or rich pastas.

Kitchen Survivor™ Grade: B+

Your notes: _____

Frog's Leap Zinfandel, Napa,   **Pts**
California 2008   **$28**   **91**

Exuberant blueberry Zin fruit, sweet spices and soft vanilla, all in balance and with a eucalyptus-wood smoke earthiness for contrast. Great with mu shu pork, spice-rubbed duck or Moroccan-spiced lamb.

Kitchen Survivor™ Grade: B

Your notes: _____

Grgich Hills Estate Zinfandel,   **Pts**
California 2007   **$30**   **93**

Zin the way it used to be, with both a yin of sweet dark fig and anise, and a yang of savory sundried tomato, black pepper and leather. A great partner for lusty, rustic dishes like Provencal lamb stew, braised short ribs or farmstead cheeses.

Kitchen Survivor™ Grade: B+

Your notes: _____

Joel Gott Zinfandel,   **Pts**
California 2008   **$14**   **88**

A "gulper" bursting with blueberry pie filling and cinnamon spice flavors. Great with chicken mole poblano and blue cheeseburgers on the grill.

Kitchen Survivor™ Grade: B+

Your notes: _____

Martinelli Vellutini Ranch Zinfandel,   **Pts**
Russian River Valley, California 2007   **$60**   **91**

Oh, the chocolate-cherry cordials and blueberry and cinnamon Pop-Tarts of youth! The lusciousness is checked by a peppery spice, so it's the "big Zin" taste without being cloying. Wonderful with dark chocolate and grilled bacon-blue cheeseburgers.

Kitchen Survivor™ Grade: B+

Your notes: _____

Ravenswood Sonoma County Old Vines   **Pts**
Zinfandel, California 2007   **$14**   **90**

An awesome Zin for the price, with loads of chewy raspberry fruit leather and smoky-spicy barbecue sauce notes. That's a slow-pitch for what to pair!

Kitchen Survivor™ Grade: B

Your notes: _____

Ridge Lytton Springs, Dry Creek Valley,   **Pts**
California 2008   **$40**   **94**

Dark blackberry, fig and sweet vanilla play off of minerally wet charcoal, pepper and tree bark earthiness. An earthy-tangy pairing of roasted beets with goat cheese sets off the sweet-savory interplay perfectly!

Kitchen Survivor™ Grade: B+

Your notes: _____

Storybook Mountain Mayacamas Range   **Pts**
Estate Zinfandel, Napa, California 2008   **$30**   **91**

Supple and succulent, with boysenberry, cinnamon and brambly molasses notes plus a luxuriant berry compote texture. Pair with BBQ, or my rockin' "Zinhead flatbread": fresh mozzarella melted on a pita with strawberries, black pepper and balsamic. Yum!

Kitchen Survivor™ Grade: B

Your notes: _____

DESSERT WINES

Category Profile: There are plenty of great and available dessert wines to choose from, many of them affordable enough to enjoy often, with or instead of dessert (they're fat free!). In this lineup there are worthy and available choices in all price points, and in all of the classic dessert wine styles: a) fortified - alcohol added to stop the sugar fermentation; b) late harvest/botrytis - picked late, and possibly infected with a sugar-concentrating mold; c) frozen-grape wines - ice wines made from grapes frozen on the vine or in a freezer before pressing; or d) dried-grape wines - made from grapes that have been dried into raisins before pressing. I hope you'll try them, because they will really jazz up your wine and food life. They are fantastic for entertaining, because they are unique and memorable, putting a distinctive mark on your dinner parties and cocktail gatherings.

Serve: Serving temperature depends on the wine, so see the individual entries.

When: With dessert, or *as* dessert; the lighter ones also make nice aperitifs. If you like to entertain, they're great. Add fruit, cheese, or some cookies, and you have a very classy end to a meal with very low hassle.

With: Blue cheese, chocolate, or simple cookies (like biscotti or shortbread) are classic.

In: The One™ glass for white wines, or an all-purpose wineglass, or smaller dessert wineglass. (The standard serving is 3 ounces rather than the traditional 5-6 ounces for most wines, because of the sugar and/or alcohol intensity typical of most dessert wines.)

Almost Top Ten Dessert Wines:

These wines are also well worth checking out.

Rivetti Moscato d'Asti
Paolo Saracco Moscato d'Asti
Inniskillin Ice Wine
Coyeaux Beaumes de Venise

"Worth the splurge" Dessert Wines:

Weinbach Selection de Grains Nobles
Chateau Suduiraut
Chateau Guiraud
Zind-Humbrecht Clos Jebsal
Quinta do Noval Colheita Porto
Dolce by Far Niente
Beringer Nightingale Late Harvest

TOP TEN DESSERT WINES

Blandy's 10-Year-Old Malmsey   **Pts**
Madeira, Portugal NV   **$33**   **92**

Caramel, burnt sugar, toffee, candied orange peel, toasted nuts, spice, and a cut of tangy acidity - that's classic Madeira (a fortified wine). Pair it with caramel or nut desserts or, best of all, dark chocolate!

Kitchen Survivor™ Grade: A+

Your notes: _____

Calem 10 Year Old Tawny Porto,   **Pts**
Oporto, Portugal NV   **$30**   **91**

An exciting Delta pick that will match our on-board cheese and fruit course as well as dessert beautifully! The heady scents and flavors of toasted pecans, toffee and nut brittle, sweet on the palate but dry and nutty on the finish, make it lovely just for sipping, too.

Kitchen Survivor™ Grade: A+

Your notes: _____

Castello Banfi Brachetto d'Acqui Rosa   **Pts**
Regale, Piedmont, Italy 2009   **$20**   **91**

The rose on the label hints at this wine's alluring rose petal scent, accented with allspice and juicy raspberry flavors on the palate. It is a love letter to chocolate truffles and also makes a great not-too-sweet aperitif.

Kitchen Survivor™ Grade: B

Your notes: _____

Chambers Rosewood Muscadelle,   **Pts**
Rutherglen, Australia NV (half bottle)   **$15**   **91**

Flavors of sweet figs, Christmas fruitcake and toffee make this like-no-other wine an exotic partner for chocolate, pecan pie or aged cheddar cheese. Mmm!

Kitchen Survivor™ Grade: A+

Your notes: _____

Chateau Coutet, Barsac-Sauternes,   **Pts**
Bordeaux, France 2007   **$52**   **93**

Botrytis mold shrivels the grapes, turning their juice to honey-mushroomy, apricot nectar. But the wine finishes almost dry, making it perfect for spicy sushi.

Kitchen Survivor™ Grade: B+

Your notes: _____

Chateau du Cros, Loupiac,   **Pts**
France 2007 (half bottle)   **$14**   **90**

I chose this for Delta because I know passengers will adore the burst of exotic floral, honeysuckle and apricot jam notes on a long flight. It's lovely with vanilla ice cream and cheeses, or just on its own.

Kitchen Survivor™ Grade: B

Your notes: _____

Chateau La Tour Blanche, Sauternes,   **Pts**
Bordeaux, France 2007   **$60**   **94**

This wine's gorgeous spice, floral and apricot layers and honeyed texture are positively extravagant. Pair with blue cheese, foie gras, aged Cheddar or just take in this triumphant FAVE bottling on its own.

Kitchen Survivor™ Grade: A+

Your notes: _____

Chateau Ste. Michelle 'Ethos' Late Harvest   **Pts**
Riesling, Washington 2006 (half bottle)   **$32**   **92**

Concentrated mango sorbet, peach pie filling and floral honeysuckle notes, are all balanced by tingly acidity, making this delicious on its own, but also great for creme brulee, ice cream, or fruit tarts.

Kitchen Survivor™ Grade: B+

Your notes: _____

Ferreira Doña Antonia Tawny Porto,   **Pts**
Oporto, Portugal NV   **$18**   **90**

The alluring toasted nut, cinnamon sugar, cappuccino, and maple scents and flavors made this a perfect Delta pick for the cheese course, dessert or both. It's also irresistible with the Delta signature Biscoff cookies (even better if you dunk 'em in the wine!). Busted!

Kitchen Survivor™ Grade: A+

Your notes: _____

Pacific Rim 'Selenium Vineyard' Riesling   **Pts**
Vin de Glaciere, Washington 2007   **$15**   **90**

A perfect Delta pick because the tingly lemon meringue pie and passion fruit flavors dazzles your palate even at altitude. Fabulous with ice cream, cheeses, fresh fruit or just for indulgent sipping.

Kitchen Survivor™ Grade: A+

Your notes: _____

HIGH-FLYING WINE: MY DELTA AIR LINES PARTNERSHIP

About four years ago I got the opportunity to work with Delta Air Lines on its Business Elite® wine program. I had done wine programs in large retail, hotel chains, casual dining and fine dining, but an airline was a new challenge so I jumped at the chance. I love any opportunity to work with wine across a broad population, and with millions of flying passengers to look after each year, I knew this was going to be a blast, and that I would learn a lot. For example *did you know*:

The best wines for serving in-flight are those with lots of flavor intensity and vibrant fruit. The reason is that your senses of taste and smell are muted at altitude. Consequently, a delicate wine that tastes great at sea-level might seem thin and watery in-flight. Throughout this guide I have noted my Delta picks and pointed out the flavor characteristics that make them especially suited for enjoyment in-flight.

Green matters. With millions of bottles of wine served in-flight each year, our choice to showcase wineries that are committed to sustainable farming practices makes a big difference. We took a further step last year toward reducing the carbon footprint of our wine program by launching Bandit Chardonnay and Merlot in Tetra® packaging for international coach class. The lighter, recyclable packaging significantly reduces the carbon impact of the wine served as compared to glass bottles. And the wine tastes great!

Wine is as global as travel itself! As such, we feature great wines from destinations both classic and cutting-edge, all around the world. Having studied all of the world's wine regions in preparation for my Master Sommelier test, I was excited for the chance to pay tribute to some of the many destinations Delta serves via our wine offerings. We are particularly focused on our home turf, of course. And since California, Oregon and Washington wines are equal in quality to the finest classic wine regions, it's fun to showcase top U.S. bottlings on our flights. We also give special attention to featuring great French wines on board, both as a tribute to our joint venture with Air France, and because the wines are world-class. (Tip: Don't miss the French Champagne poured on every Business Elite® flight. It's *magnifique*.)

When it comes to in-flight wine and food pairings, our customers weigh in, too! For the second year in a row, the Delta In-Flight Service team, consulting chef Michelle Bernstein, and I have convened a panel of our elite frequent flyers to taste our finalist wine selections with some of Michelle's newest culinary creations, and help us decide the best pairing match-ups for our menu rotations. (I know, tough job but someone's got to do it!). Let us know how we're doing ok?

And now...Meet Delta's Flying Sommeliers!

Tens of thousands of Flight Attendants, plus millions of bottles of wine, equals happy customers, right? We hope so! I've always believed that to know wine is to love it, and as a sommelier I also know that serving wine is a lot more fun if you know a little something about each selection and the region it hails from that you can share with your guest. So, in addition providing the tasting and pairing notes on the following pages to our flight attendants, we are also launching a training program adapted from the video wine course on my website, Andreawine.com. Check it out and see all the cool videos. Maybe you'll want to follow along, too!

Will there be a test? Flight Attendants will be able to test their knowledge with fun online quizzes. Maybe there will even be a "winged corkscrew" pin for those who really master the juice (haven't worked that part out yet!).

Delta Business Elite® Wines for 2011

Here is a list of the wine selections that will be served in Delta Business Elite® throughout the year beginning in February 2011.

Sparkling & Champagne

Veuve du Vernay Brut, France NV—This wine's deep, Champagne-like brioche and apple tart flavors and length on the finish are absolutely amazing. A fabulous match for aged cheeses, warm nuts and other salty snacks.

Champagne Jacquart Brut Mosaique, France NV—The sommelier at Air France tipped me off to this wonderful bubbly. I chose it because the rich scents of poundcake and brioche and the spicy apple compote flavors will stand out in-flight. Delicious with those warm nuts at the beginning of the meal, but don't forget to ask for a glass to go with the cheese course, too!

White

Sonoma-Cutrer Russian River Ranches Chardonnay, California—This is one of the most famous California Chardonnays, for good reason. The intense stone fruit and pineapple flavors and soft vanilla oakiness are delicious just for sipping, as well as for pairing with poultry, seafood, pasta or spicy dishes. It's also great with cheese.

Le Charme de Marjosse, Bordeaux, France—A gorgeous white Bordeaux blend of Sauvignon Blanc and Semillon grapes, tangy with key lime flavors, plus juicy melon and a honeyed creaminess from the oak aging. Great with seafood, salads, pastas and cheese.

St. Supery Sauvignon Blanc, Napa, California—One of California's most famous Sauvignon Blancs from the famed Napa region! This wine's exotic fennel, fig and grilled pineapple notes, and the citrus tanginess, will shine at altitude and pair great with anything from salad to pasta to smoked salmon.

Gougenheim Torrontes, Mendoza, Argentina—This wine is an explosion of tropical, floral and exotic citrus notes (think kumquat and tangerine). It is so delicious on its own, but also a great partner for spicy fare, salads, smoked salmon and seafood.

Mer Soleil 'Silver' Chardonnay, Monterey, California — From the famous Wagner family - owners of Napa's Caymus Vineyards who also own top vineyards in Monterey. The no-holds-barred pineapple-mango fruit in this wine tastes like a trip to Hawaii (or at least, Trader Vic's!) in a glass. "Silver" refers to the stainless steel fermentation tanks used (instead of oak barrels) so all that fruit can shine through. Great just for sipping, and with salads, smoked salmon, Asian and spicy fare.

Zalze 'Bush Vine' Chenin Blanc, South Africa—Look up "exotic" in the dictionary and you might see this label. The wine is opulent with buttercream, apricot, honey and golden pineapple flavors. So delicious on its own, but also with salty snacks, smoked salmon, salads, seafood, pastas, even cheese!

Domaine Vincent Girardin Pouilly-Fuissé Vieilles Vignes, Burgundy, France—Vieilles Vignes or "old vines," yield lots of complexity: lovely wet stone minerality, and scents of apple peel and white blossoms. All those layers, and the lively acidity, will show beautifully even at 30,000 feet, solo or with food - especially seafood, salads, pastas and cheeses.

Chakana Yaguarete Collection Torrontes, Mendoza, Argentina—A tropical fruit salad-in-a-glass, with honeysuckle floral notes and juicy, mouthwatering acidity. It's a delicious sipper, and a great match for spicy fare, pastas, seafood and smoked salmon.

Red

Cousino-Macul Antiguas Reservas Cabernet Sauvignon, Chile - Dusty tobacco, mushrooms, leather and dark berry fruit make this one of the most complex Cabs out there. All those exotic layers and the velvety texture will make it a standout wine at altitude, and a delicious match for pastas, beef filet and cheeses.

Red (cont.)

Albert Bichot Mercurey, Burgundy, France - A classic French Burgundy, with great complexity: lots of savory smoke, white pepper, cumin and cranberry notes, framed by soft vanilla scents from oak aging. It will be a fantastic match for pastas, fish, meat dishes and fine cheeses.

Bodegas Bordon Rioja Gran Reserva, Spain—It's exciting to have a bottle-aged pick like this for our "cellar in the sky" because the bewitching leather, mushrooms, meat stock, tobacco, dark spiced figs and satin texture make it a truly special tasting experience. A great partner for poultry, beef and of course, the cheese course!

Antu Ninquén Cabernet Sauvignon-Carmenere by MontGras, Colchagua, Chile—This is a head-turner red with bewitching cumin, smoke and consomme notes, ripe crushed plum fruit and a velvety-rich texture. It will pair well with anything from cheesy pastas to a velvety beef filet.

Robert Mondavi Carneros Pinot Noir, Napa, California—From one of the most famous names in wine comes this amazing Pinot. I love the yin-yang of savory-sweet notes - fennel seed, black licorice, roasted plum - and the satiny texture. A stunning match with fish, pastas, meat dishes and especially, the Moroccan spices that Chef Michelle Bernstein loves to weave into her Delta culinary creations.

Chakana Estate Malbec, Mendoza, Argentina—Sumptuous fig and blackberry fruit, dark chocolate and anise notes, and a liquefied velvet texture - what's not to love? Fantastic with meat dishes, cheesy pastas and fine cheeses.

Chateau Beaumont, Haut-Medoc, Bordeaux, France - Classic Bordeaux style *par excellence*: pencil dust, cedar, leafy earthiness, blackcurrant fruit and a mocha finish. Pairs well with all but light fish dishes, and be sure to keep a splash in your glass for the cheese course!

Meiomi by Belle Glos Pinot Noir, Sonoma Coast, California— Belle Glos Pinot Noirs (from the owners of Caymus) are all the buzz. This wine shows alluring scents of sweet balsamic, dark cherries, hoisin sauce and baking spices that are a sensory treat on their own, and with salmon, meat dishes, pastas and cheeses. Meiomi (may-OH-mee) means "coast" - the best place to grow Pinot Noir in California - in the local Wappo and Yuki tribal dialect.

Dessert

Chateau du Cros, Loupiac, Bordeaux, France - Prepare to be smitten! You will adore this wine's burst of exotic floral, honeysuckle and apricot jam notes. It's lovely with vanilla ice cream and cheeses, or just on its own.

Pacific Rim Selenium Vineyard Riesling 'Vin de Glaciere', Washington - The tingly lemon meringue pie and passion fruit flavors in this wine will dazzle your palate even at altitude. Fabulous with ice cream, cheeses, fresh fruit or just for indulgent sipping. Vin de Glaciere or "glacier wine" is a tongue-in-cheek reference to the fact that the grapes are frozen before pressing, to concentrate the sweetness and fruit intensity.

Ferreira Dona Antonia Reserve Porto, Portugal—Alluring toasted nut, cinnamon sugar, cappuccino, and maple scents and flavors make this a perfect wine for the cheese course, dessert or both. It's also irresistible with the Delta signature Biscoff cookies (even better if you dunk 'em in the wine!). Busted!

Calem 10 Year Old Tawny Porto, Portugal— This wine will match our on-board cheese and fruit course, as well as dessert, beautifully! The heady scents and flavors of toasted pecans, toffee and nut brittle, sweet on the palate but dry and nutty on the finish, make it lovely just for sipping, too.

Happy sipping, and happy traveling!

THE
COMPLETE WINE COURSE
MINI-COURSE:
A WINE CLASS IN A GLASS

How do you go about choosing wine? The best way to ensure you'll be happy with your wine choices is to learn your taste.

Here are two quick wine lessons, adapted from my *Complete Wine Course DVD,* that will let you do exactly that. You're probably thinking, Will there be a test? In a way, every pulled cork is a test, but for the *wine:* Are you happy with what you got for the price you paid, and would you buy it again? This mini-course will teach you to pick wines that pass muster by helping you learn what styles and tastes you like in a wine and how to use the label to help you find them.

If you want, you can complete each lesson in a matter of minutes. As with food, tasting impressions form quickly with wine. Then you can get dinner on the table, accompanied by your wine picks. Start by doing the first lesson, "White Wine Made Simple," one evening, and then Lesson 2, "Red Wine Made Simple," another time. Or you can invite friends over and make it a party. Everyone will learn a little bit about wine, while having fun.

Setup
Glassware: You will need three glasses per taster. A simple all-purpose wineglass is ideal, but clear disposables are fine, too.

Pouring: Start with a tasting portion (about an ounce of each wine). Tasters can re-pour more of their favorite to enjoy with hors d'oeuvres or dinner.

Flights: Taste the Lesson 1 whites first and then the Lesson 2 reds (pros call each sequence of wine a *flight*). There is no need to wash or rinse the glasses.

To Taste It Is to Know It
Tasting is the fastest way to learn about wine. My wine students tell me this all the time: They know

what wines they like when they try them. The trick is in understanding the style and knowing how to ask for it and get it again: "I'd like a Chardonnay with lots of buttery, toasty oak and gobs of creamy, tropical fruit flavors." If you don't know what it means, you might feel silly offering a description like that when wine shopping. But those words really are in the glass, and these easy-to-follow tasting lessons will help you recognize the styles and learn which ones are your favorites.

The Lessons

What You'll Do:

For Lesson 1, "White Wine Made Simple," you will comparison-taste three major white wine grapes: Riesling, Sauvignon Blanc, and Chardonnay. For Lesson 2, "Red Wine Made Simple," you will compare three major reds: Pinot Noir, Merlot, and Cabernet Sauvignon. Follow these easy steps:

1. Buy your wines. Make your choice from the varietal sections of this book. It's best to choose wines in the same price category—for example, all under-$15 wines.
2. Chill (even the reds can take a light chill; they warm up quickly and can taste out of balance if too warm), pour, and taste the wines in the order of body, light to full, as shown in the tasting notes.
3. Use the tasting notes as a guide, and record your own if you want.

What You'll Learn:

Body styles of the major grapes—light, medium, or full. You'll see that Riesling is lighter (less heavy) than Chardonnay, in the same way that, for example, skim milk is lighter than heavy cream.

What the major grapes taste like—When tasted side by side, the grapes are quite distinctive, just as a pear tastes different from an apple, a strawberry tastes different from a blueberry, and so on.

What other wine flavor words taste like—Specifically, you'll experience these tastes: oaky, tannic, crisp, and fruity. Knowing them is helpful because they're used a lot in this book, on wine bottle labels, and by sellers of wine—merchants, waiters, and so on.

Getting comfortable with these basics will equip you to describe the wine styles you like to a waiter or wine merchant and to use the information on a bottle label to find those styles on your own. In the "Buying Lingo" section that follows, I've defined lots of other style words and listed some wine types you can try to experience them.

Tasting Lesson 1
WHITE WINE MADE SIMPLE

Instructions: Taste the wines in numbered order. Note your impressions of:

Color: Which is lightest and which is darkest? Whites can range from pale straw to deep yellow-gold. The darker the color, the fuller the body.

Scent: While they all smell like white wine, the aromas differ, from delicate and tangy to rich and fruity.

Taste and Body: In the same way that fruits range from crisp and tart (like apples) to ripe and lush (like mangoes), the wine tastes will vary along with the body styles of the grapes, from light to full.

Which grape and style do you like best? If you like more than one style, that's great, too!

The White Wines

Grape 1: Riesling (any region)—light bodied

Description: Crisp and refreshing, with vibrant fruit flavor ranging from apple to peach.

Brand name:_____

Your notes: _____

_____

Grape 2: Sauvignon Blanc (France or New Zealand)—medium bodied

Description: Very distinctive! The smell is exotically pungent, the taste tangy and mouthwatering, like citrus fruit (lime and grapefruit).

Brand name:_____

Your notes: _____

_____

Grape 3: Chardonnay (California)—full bodied

Description: The richest scent and taste, with fruit flavor ranging from ripe apples to peaches to tropical fruits. You can feel the full-bodied texture, too. "Oaky" scents come through as a sweet, buttery, or toasty impression.

Brand name: _____

Your notes: _____

_____

Tasting Lesson 2
RED WINE MADE SIMPLE

Instructions: Again, taste the wines in numbered order and note your impressions.

Color: Red wines range in color from transparent ruby, like the Pinot Noir, to inky dark purple—the darker the color, the fuller the body.

Scent: In addition to the smell of "red wine," you'll get the cherrylike smell of Pinot Noir, perhaps plum character in the Merlot, and a rich dark-berry smell in the Cabernet. There are other scents, too, so enjoy them. You can also compare your impressions with those included in the reviews section of the book.

Taste and Body: Like white wines, red wines range from light and delicate to rich and intense. You'll note the differences in body from light to full and the distinctive taste character of each grape. As you can see, tasting them side by side makes it easy to detect and compare the differences.

The Red Wines

Grape 1: Pinot Noir (any region)—light bodied

Description: Delicate cherrylike fruit flavor, silky-smooth texture, mouthwatering acidity, all of which make Pinot Noir a versatile wine for most types of food.

Brand name: _____

Your notes: _____

_____

Grape 2: Merlot/Cabernet Sauvignon (California, Chile, or Washington)—medium-to-full bodied

Description: More intense than Pinot Noir, with rich plum and blackberry flavors. Notice the drying sensation it leaves on your tongue? That's tannin, a natural grape component that, like color, comes from the skin. As you can see, more color and more tannin come together. Tasting high-tannin wines with fat or protein counters that drying sensation (that's why Cabernet and red meat are considered classic partners). In reds, an "oaky" character comes through as one or more of these scents: spice, cedar, smoke, toastiness, vanilla, and coconut. No wonder buyers love it!

Brand name: _____

Your notes: _____

_____

Grape 3: Syrah/Shiraz (Australia, California, Washington or Rhone)—full bodied

Description: Dark fruit (plums and berries) like Merlot and Cabernet, and plenty of tannin gripping your tongue. There is often a black pepper-spicy quality and intense flavor concentration. The alcohol level can also be higher, adding to the impression of full body.

Brand name: _____

Your notes: _____

_____

Wine Glossary

Here are the meanings of some of the major wine style words that you see in this book, on wine bottles and in wine shops.

Acidity—The tangy, tart, crisp, mouthwatering component in wine. It's a prominent characteristic of Riesling, Sauvignon Blanc, and Pinot Grigio whites and Pinot Noir and Chianti/Sangiovese reds.

Bag-in-a-Box—A box with a wine-filled bag inside that deflates as the wine is consumed, preventing oxidation.

Balance—The harmony of all the wine's main components: fruit, alcohol, and acidity, plus sweetness (if any), oak (if used in the wine making), and tannin (in reds). As with food, balance in the wine is important to your enjoyment, and a sign of quality. But it's also a matter of taste—the dish may taste "too salty" and the wine "too oaky" for one person but be fine to another.

Barrel aged / barrel fermented—The wine was aged or fermented (or both) in oak barrels. The barrels give fuller body as well as an "oaky" character to the wine's scent and flavor, making it seem richer. "Oaky" scents are often in the sweet family—but *not* sugary. Rather, *toasty, spicy, vanilla, buttery,* and *coconut* are the common wine words to describe "oaky" character. Other label signals that mean "oaky": Barrel Fermented, Barrel Select, Barrel Cuvee, Cask Fermented.

Bouquet—All of the wine's scents, which come from the grape(s) used, the techniques (like oak aging), the age of the wine, and the vineyard characteristics (like soil and climate).

Bright—Vivid and vibrant. Usually used as a modifier, like "bright fruit" or "bright acidity."

Buttery—Literally, the creamy-sweet smell of butter. One by-product of fermentation is an ester that mimics the butter smell, so you may well notice this in some wines, especially barrel-fermented Chardonnays.

Corked, corky—Refers to a wine whose scent or taste has been tainted by corks or wine-making equipment infected with a bacteria called TCA. While not harmful to health, TCA gives wines a musty smell and taste.

Creamy—Can mean a smell similar to fresh cream or a smooth and lush texture. In sparkling wines, it's a textural delicacy and smoothness of the bubbles.

Crisp—See ACIDITY.

Dry—A wine without sweetness (though not without fruit; see FRUITY for more on this).

Earthy—As with cheeses, potatoes, mushrooms, and other good consumables, wines can have scents and flavors reminiscent of, or owing to, the soil. The "earth" terms commonly attributed to wine include *mushrooms, truffles, flint, dusty, gravelly, chalky, slaty, wet leaves,* and even *barnyard.*

Exotic—Just as it applies to other things, this description suggests unusual and alluring characteristics in wine. Quite often refers to wines with a floral or spicy style or flavors beyond your typical fruit bowl, such as tropical fruits or rare berries.

Floral—Having scents that mimic flower scents, whether fresh (as in the honeysuckle scent of some Rieslings) or dried (as in the wilted rose petal scent of some Gewürztraminers).

Food friendly—Food-friendly wines have taste characteristics that pair well with a wide variety of foods without clashing or overpowering—namely, good acidity and moderate (not too heavy) body. The food-friendly whites include Riesling and Sauvignon Blanc; the reds include Chianti, Spanish Rioja, red Rhone, and Pinot Noir wines.

Fruity—Marked by a prominent smell and taste of fruit. In whites the fruit tastes can range from lean and tangy (like lemons and crisp apples) to medium (like melons and peaches) to lush (like mangoes and pineapples). In reds, think cranberries and cherries, plums and blueberries, figs and prunes. Note that *fruity* doesn't mean "sweet." The taste and smell of ripe fruit are perceived as sweet, but they're not sugary. Most wines on the market are at once dry (meaning not sweet) and fruity, with lots of fruit flavor.

Grassy—Describes a wine marked with scents of fresh-cut grass or herbs or even green vegetables (like green pepper and asparagus). It's a signature of Sauvignon Blanc wines, especially those grown in New Zealand and France. *Herbal* and *herbaceous* are close synonyms.

Herbal, herbaceous—See GRASSY.

Legs—The drips running down the inside of the wineglass after you swirl it. Not a sign of quality (as in "good legs") but of viscosity. Fast-running legs indicate a low-viscosity wine and slow legs a high-viscosity wine. The higher the viscosity, the richer and fuller the wine feels in your mouth.

Nose—The smell of the wine. Isn't it interesting how wines have a nose, legs, and body? As you've no doubt discovered, they have personalities, too!

Oaky—See BARREL AGED.

Off-dry—A lightly sweet wine.

Old vines—Refers to wine from vines significantly older than average, usually at least 30 years old and sometimes far older. Older vines yield a smaller, but often more intensely flavored, crop of grapes.

Regional wine—A wine named for the region where the grapes are grown, such as Champagne, Chianti, and Pouilly-Fuisse.

Spicy—A wine with scents and flavors reminiscent of spices, both sweet (cinnamon, ginger, cardamom, clove) and savory (pepper, cumin, curry).

Sweet—A wine that has perceptible sugar, called *residual sugar* because it is left over from fermentation and not converted to alcohol. A wine can be lightly sweet like a Moscato or very sweet like a Port or Sauternes.

Tannic—A red wine whose tannin is noticeable—a little or a lot—as a drying sensation on your tongue ranging from gentle (lightly tannic) to velvety (richly tannic) to harsh (too tannic).

Terroir—The distinctive flavors, scents, and character of a wine owing to its vineyard source. For example, the terroir of French red Burgundies is sometimes described as *earthy*.

Toasty—Wines with a toasty, roasted, caramelized, or smoky scent reminiscent of coffee beans, toasted nuts or spices, or burnt sugar.

Unfiltered—A wine that has not been filtered before bottling (which is common practice). Some say filtering the wine strips out flavor, but not everyone agrees. I think most tasters cannot tell the difference.

Varietal wine—A wine named for the grape used to make it, such as Chardonnay or Merlot.

Handling Wine Leftovers

I developed the Kitchen Survivor™ grades to give you an idea of how long each wine stays in good drinking condition if you don't finish the bottle. In the same way that resealing the cereal box or wrapping and refrigerating leftovers will extend their freshness window, you can do the same for wine by handling the leftovers as follows:

Still Wines

Re-cork—At a minimum, close the bottle with its original cork. Most wines will stay fresh a day or two at normal room temperature. To extend that freshness-window, purchase a vacuum-sealer (available in kitchenware shops and wine shops). You simply cork the bottle with the purchased rubber stopper, which has a one-way valve. The accompanying plastic vacuum pump is then placed on top of the stopper; you pump the handle repeatedly until the resistance tightens, indicating the air has been pumped out of the bottle. (Note: A few wine experts don't think rubber stoppers work, but I have used them for years. In my restaurants, I have found they extended the life of bottles opened for by-the-glass service at least two days longer than just sealing with the original cork.)

Refrigerate stoppered (and vacuum-sealed) bottles, whether white, pink, or red. Refrigeration of anything slows the spoilage, and your red wine, once removed from the fridge and poured in the glass, will quickly come to serving temperature.

For even longer shelf-life, you can preserve partial bottles with inert gas. I recommend this especially for more expensive wines. Wine Life and Private Preserve are two brands that I have used (sold in wine shops and accessories catalogs). They come in a can that feels light, as if it were empty. Inside is an inert gas mixture that is heavier than air. The can's spray nozzle is inserted into the bottle. A one-second spray fills the empty bottle space with the inert gas, displacing the air inside, which is the key because no air in contact with the wine means no oxidation. Then you quickly replace the cork (make sure the fit is tight). My experience in restaurants using gas systems for very upscale wines by the glass is that they keep well for a week or more.

Sparkling Wines

Your best bet is to purchase "clam shell" Champagne stoppers, with one or two hinged metal clamps attached to a stopper top that has a rubber or plastic gasket for a tight seal. You place the stopper on top, press down, and then anchor the clamps to the bottle lip. If you open your sparkler carefully and don't "pop" the cork, losing precious carbonation, a stoppered partial bottle will keep its effervescence for at least a few days, and sometimes much longer.

SAVVY SHOPPER: RETAIL WINE BUYING

Supermarkets, pharmacies, price clubs, catalogs, state stores, mega-stores, dot.coms, and boutiques . . . where you shop for wine depends a lot on the state where you live, because selling wine requires a state license. What many people don't realize is how much the wine laws vary from one state to the next.

In most states, the regulations affect the prices you pay for wine, what wines are available, and how you get your hands on them (ideally, they are delivered to your door or poured at your table, but this isn't always legal). Here is a quick summary of the retail scene to help you make the most of your buying power wherever you live.

Wine Availability The single biggest frustration for every wine buyer and winery is bureaucracy. To ensure the collection of excise taxes, in nearly all states every single wine must be registered and approved in some way before it can be sold. If a wine you're seeking isn't available in your area, this is probably the reason. For many small boutique wineries, it just isn't worth the bother and expense to get legal approval for the few cases of wine they would sell in a particular state. One extreme example is Pennsylvania, a "control state" where wine is sold exclusively by a state-run monopoly that, without competition, has little incentive to source a lot of boutique wines. By contrast, California, New York, and Chicago, with high demand and competition, are good markets for wine availability.

Wine Prices and Discounts Wine prices can vary from one state to the next due to different tax rates. And in general, prices are lower in competitive markets, where stores can use discounts, sale prices, and so on to vie for your business.

Where they are legal, case discounts of 10% to 15% are a great way to get the best possible prices for your favorite wines. On the more expensive wines, many people I know coordinate their buying with friends and family so they can buy full cases and get these discounts.

Delivery and Wine-by-Mail In many states, it is not legal for stores or other retailers to deliver wine to the purchaser.

Many catalogs and Web sites sell wine by mail. Some are affiliated with retail stores or wineries, whereas others are strictly virtual stores. The conveniences include shopping on your own time and terms, from home or office, helpful buying recommendations and information, and usually home delivery. Keep in mind that the laws governing such shipping are complex, and vary from state to state (in some states it is completely prohibited).

Mail-order wine clubs are an interesting option when you are looking for new wines to try. For information on my own wine club, Andrea's A-List,™ visit my Web site, www.andreawine.com.

Where Should I Shop? That depends on what you're buying. If you know what you want, then price is your main consideration, and you'll get your best deals at venues that concentrate on volume sales— discount stores, price clubs, and so on. If you want buying advice, or are buying rare wines, you're better off in a wine shop or merchant specializing in collectible wines. These stores have trained buyers who taste and know their inventory well; they can help you with your decision. The better stores also have temperature-controlled storage for their rare wines, which is critical to ensure you get a product in good condition. There are also Web-based fine and rare wine specialists, but that is a fairly new market. I suggest you purchase fine and rare wines only through sources with a good track record of customer service. In that way, if you have problems with a shipment, you will have some recourse.

Can I Take That Bottle on the Wine List Home with Me? In most states, restaurants' wine licenses allow for sale and consumption "on-premise" only, meaning they cannot sell you a bottle to take home.

Burgundy Buyers, Beware With the exception of volume categories such as Beaujolais, Macon, and

Pouilly-Fuissé, buyers of French white and red Burgundy should shop only at fine wine merchants, preferably those that specialize in Burgundy, for two reasons. First, Burgundy is simply too fragile to handle the storage conditions in most stores. Burgundy specialists ensure temperature-controlled storage. Second, selection is a major factor, because quality varies a lot from one winery to the next, and from one vintage to the next. Specialist stores have the needed buying expertise to ensure the quality of their offerings.

Is That a Deal or a Disaster? Floor stacks, "end caps," private labels, and bin ends can be a boon for the buyer, or a bust, depending on where you are shopping. Here's what you need to know about them:

"Floor Stacks" of large-volume categories and brands (e.g., branded varietal wines)—These are a best bet in supermarkets and other volume-based venues, where they're used to draw your attention to a price markdown. Take advantage of it to stock up for everyday or party wines.

"End Cap" wine displays featured at the ends of aisles—A good bet, especially in fine wine shops. You may not have heard of the wine, but they're usually "hidden gems" that the buyer discovered and bought in volume, to offer you quality and uniqueness at a savings.

"Bin Ends"—Retailers often clear out the last few bottles of something by discounting the price. In reputable retail stores, they are usually still good quality, and thus a good bet. Otherwise, steer clear.

Private labels—These are wines blended and bottled exclusively for the retailer—again, good bets in reputable stores, who stake their reputation on your satisfaction with their private labels.

"Shelf-talkers"—Written signs, reviews, and ratings. Good shops offer their own recommendations in lieu of, or along with, critics' scores. If the only information is a critic's score, check to be sure that the vintage being sold matches that of the wine that was reviewed.

BUYING WINE IN RESTAURANTS

Wine List Strategy Session

A lot of us have a love–hate relationship with the wine list. On the one hand, we know it holds the potential to enhance the evening, impress the date or client, broaden our horizons, or all three. But it also makes us feel intimidated, inadequate, overwhelmed, and . . .

Panicked by prices—That goes for both the cheapest wines *and* the most expensive ones; we're leery of extremes.

Pressured by pairing—Will this wine "go with" our food?

Overwhelmed by options—Can this wine I've never heard of possibly be any good? Does my selection measure up? (Remember, the restaurant is supposed to impress *you,* not the other way around.) This "phone book" wine list makes me want to dial 911.

Stumped by Styles—Food menus are easy because we understand the key terms: appetizer, entree, dessert, salad, soup, fish, meat, and so on. But after *white* and *red,* most of us get lost pretty quickly with wine categories. (Burgundy . . . is that a style, a color, a place, or all three?)

Let's deal with the first three above. For the lowdown on wine list terms, use the decoder that follows to pinpoint the grapes and styles behind all the major wine names.

Wine List Prices

The prices on wine lists reflect three things:

- *The dining-out experience*—The restaurant wine markup is higher than in retail stores because the decor is (usually) nicer, and you get to stay a while, during which time they open the wine, serve it in a nice glass, and clean up afterward. They also may have invested in the cost and expertise to select and store the wine properly. Consequently those who enjoy drinking wine in restaurants are accustomed to being charged more for the wine than you would pay to drink the same bottle at home. That said, exorbitant mark-ups are, in my opinion, the biggest deterrent to more guests enjoying wine in restaurants (which is both good for the guests and good for business). You can always vote with your wallet and dine in restaurants with guest-friendly wine pricing.

- *Location*—Restaurants in exclusive resorts, in urban centers with a business clientele, or with a star chef behind them, tend toward higher wine markups, because they can get away with it. The logic, so to speak, is that if you're on vacation, it's on the company, or it's just the "in" place, high markups (on everything) are part of the price of admission. However, I don't really think that's right, and I do think these places would sell more wine with lower markups.

- *The rarity of the wine*—Often, the rarer the wine (either because it's in high demand due to crit-ics' hype or because it's old and just a few bottles remain), the higher the markup. It's a form of rationing in the face of high demand/low supply. Food can be the same way (lobsters, truffles, caviar, etc.).

Getting the Most Restaurant Wine for Your Money

Seeking value doesn't make you a cheapskate. Here are the best strategies to keep in mind:

1. Take the road less traveled—Chardonnay and Cabernet Sauvignon are what I call "comfort wines" because they're so well known. But their prices often reflect a "comfort premium" (in the same way that a name-brand toothpaste costs more than the store brand). These spec-tacular wine styles often give better value for the money, because they're less widely known:

   Whites
   Riesling
   Sauvignon Blanc and Fume Blanc
   Sancerre (a French Loire Valley wine made
      from the Sauvignon Blanc grape)

Anything from Washington State or New Zealand

Reds
Cotes-du-Rhone and other French Rhone
   Valley reds
Red Zinfandel from California
Spanish Rioja and other reds from Spain
Cabernet Sauvignon from Chile

2. Savvy Splurging—There's no doubt about it: nothing commemorates, celebrates, or impresses better than a special wine. Since splurging on wine in a restaurant can mean especially big bucks, here are the "trophy" wine styles that give you the most for your money on wine lists:

> French Champagne—I think that Champagne (the real stuff from France's Champagne region) is among the most affordable luxuries on the planet, and its wine list prices are often among the best of all the "badge" wine categories (such as French Bordeaux and Burgundy, cult California Cabernets, and boutique Italian wines).

> California's Blue Chip Cabernets—I don't mean the tiny-production cult-movement Cabernets but rather the classics that have been around for decades, and still make world-class wine at a fair price. Names like Beringer, BV, Franciscan, Mt. Veeder, Robert Mondavi, Silver Oak, and Stag's Leap all made the Top Ten, and for good reason: they're excellent and available.

> Italian Chianti Classico Riserva—This recommendation may surprise you, but I include it because the quality for the price is better than ever, and recent vintages have been great. I also think that across the country a lot of people celebrate and do business in steak houses and Italian restaurants, which tend to carry this wine category because it complements their food.

3. The Mid-price/Mid-style "Safety Zone"—This is a strategy I first developed not for dining guests but for our *waiters* trying to help diners choose a bottle, usually with very little to go on (many people aren't comfortable describing their taste preference, and they rarely broadcast their budget for fear of looking cheap). The mid-price/mid-style strategy is this: in any wine list category (e.g., Chardonnays and Italian reds), if you go for the mid-price range in that section, odds are good the wine will be mid-style. Mid-style is my shorthand for the most typical, crowd-pleasing version, likely to satisfy a high proportion of guests and to be sticker shock free. The fact is that the more expensive the wine is, the more distinctive and even unusual its style is likely to be. If it's not to your taste *and* you've spent a lot, you're doubly disappointed.

4. Ask—With wine more popular than ever, restaurants are the most proactive they've ever been in seeking to put quality and value on their wine lists. So ask for it: "What's the best red wine deal on your list right now?" Or, if you have a style preference, say something like "We want to spend $XX. Which of these Chardonnays do you think is the best for the money?"

Pairing Wine and Food

Worrying a lot about this is a big waste of time, because most wines complement most foods, regardless of wine color, center-of-the-plate protein, and all that other stuff. How well? Their affinity can range from "fine" to "Omigod." You can pretty much expect at least a nice combination every time you have wine with food and great matches from time to time (of course, frequent experimentation ups your odds). The point is, your style preference is a lot more important than the pairing, per se, because if you hate the dish or the wine, you're hardly likely to enjoy the pairing. That said, here is a list of wine styles that are especially favored by sommeliers and chefs for their exceptional food affinity and versatility, along with a few best-bet food recommendations:

Favorite "Food Wines" *White*	Best-Bet Food Matches
Champagne and Sparkling Wine—So many people save bubbly just for toasts, but it's an amazing "food wine"	Sushi All shellfish Cheeses (even stinky ones) Omelets and other egg dishes Mushroom sauces (on risotto, pasta or whatever)
Riesling from Germany, Alsace (France), America, Australia	Mexican, southwestern, and other spicy foods Shellfish Cured meats and sausages
Alsace (France) White Wines—Riesling, Pinot Gris, and Gewurztraminer	Pacific Rim foods—Japanese, Thai, Korean, Chinese Indian food Smoked meats and charcuterie Meat stews (really!)
Sauvignon Blanc and wines made from it (French Sancerre, Pouilly-Fume, and white Bordeaux)	Goat cheese Salads Herbed sauces (like pesto) Tomato dishes (salads, soups, sauces)

Red	
Beaujolais (from France)	Mushroom dishes
Pinot Noir	Fish (especially rich ones like tuna, salmon, and cod) Smoked meats Grilled vegetables Duck
Chianti, Rosso di Montalcino, and other Italian reds made from the Sangiovese grape	Pizza, eggplant parmigiana (and other Italian-American–inspired tastes) Cheesy dishes Spicy sausages
Rioja from Spain	Roasted and grilled meats

Choosing from the Wine List

You've got the wine list. Unless you know a lot about wine, you now face at least one of these dilemmas:

- You've never heard of any of the wines listed or at least none of those in your price range. (Okay, maybe you've heard of Dom Pérignon, but let's be real.) Or the names you do recognize don't interest you.

- You have no idea how much a decent selection should cost. But you *do* know you want to keep to your budget, without broadcasting it to your guests and the entire dining room.
- The wine list is so huge you don't even want to open it.

Wine List Playbook

Remember, you're the buyer. Good restaurants want you to enjoy wine and to feel comfortable with the list, your budget, and so on. As far as the wine-snobby ones go, what are you doing there anyway? (Okay, if you took a gamble on a new place or somebody else picked it, the strategies here can help.)

The basics:

1. *Don't worry if you haven't heard of the names.* There are literally thousands of worthy wines beyond the big brand names, and many restaurants feature them to spice up their selection.
2. *Determine what you want to spend.* I think most people want the best deal they can get. With that in mind, here are some price/value rules of thumb. In most restaurants the wine prices tend to relate to the food prices, as follows:
   - Wines by-the-glass: The price window for good-quality wines that please a high percentage of diners usually parallels the restaurant's mid- to top-priced appetizers. So if the Caesar salad (or wings or whatever) is $5.95, expect to spend that, plus or minus a dollar or two, for a good glass of wine. This goes for dessert wine, too. Champagne and sparkling wines can be more, due to the cost of the product and greater waste because it goes flat.
   - Bottles: This is far more variable, but in general most restaurants try to offer an ample selection of good-quality bottles priced in what I call a "selling zone" that's benchmarked to their highest entree price, plus a margin. That's the variable part. It can range from $5–10 on average in national chain restaurants and their peers to at least $10–20 in luxury and destination restaurants. So if the

casual chain's steak-and-shrimp-scampi combo costs $17.95, the $20–30 zone on their wine list will likely hold plenty of good bottle choices. In an urban restaurant where the star chef's signature herb-crusted lamb costs $28, you could expect a cluster of worthy bottles in the $35–55 range.

We in the trade find it funny, and nearly universal, that guests shy away from the least expensive wines on our lists, suspicious that there's something "wrong" with the wine. But any restaurant that's committed to wine, whether casual chain or destination eatery, puts extra effort into finding top-quality wines at the lowest price points. They may come from grapes or regions you don't know, but my advice is to muster your sense of adventure and try them. In the worst-case scenario, you'll be underwhelmed, but since tastes vary, this can happen with wine at any price. I think the odds are better that you'll enjoy one of the best deals on the wine list.

The wine list transaction: You've set your budget. Now it's time to zero in on a selection. You've got two choices—go it alone or ask for help. In either case, here's what to do:

1. Ask for the wine list right away. It's a pet peeve of mine that guests even *need* to ask (rather than getting the list automatically with the food menus), because that can cause both service delays and anxiety. Many people are scared to request the list for fear it "commits" them to a purchase, before they can determine whether they'll be comfortable with the prices and choices available. As you're being handed the menus, say "We'll take a look at the wine list, too" to indicate you want a copy to review, not a pushy sales job. *Tip:* I always ask that the wine-by-the-glass list be brought, too. Since many places change them often, they may be on a separate card or a specials board. (I think verbal listings are the worst, because often key information, like the price or winery, can get lost in translation.)

2. Determine any style particulars you're in the mood for:
   - White or red?
   - A particular grape, region, or body style?

   If the table can't reach a consensus, look at wine-by-the-glass and half-bottle options. This can happen when preferences differ or food choices are all over the map ("I'm having the oysters, he's having the wild boar, we want one wine . . ." is a stumper I've actually faced!).

3. Find your style zone in the list. Turn to the section that represents your chosen category—e.g., whites, the wine-by-the-glass section, Chardonnays, Italian reds, or whatever—or let the server know what style particulars you have in mind.

4. Match your budget. Pick a wine priced accordingly, keeping in mind these "safety zones":
   - The wines recommended in this book
   - Winery or region names that you remember liking or hearing good things about (e.g., Chianti in Italy or a different offering from your favorite white Zinfandel producer)
   - The mid-price/mid-style zone (as I explained earlier, many lists have this "sweet spot" of well-made, moderately priced offerings)
   - Featured wine specials, if they meet your price parameters

   You can communicate your budget while keeping your dignity with this easy trick I teach waiters:
   - Find your style zone—e.g., Pinot Grigios—in the wine list.
   - With both you and the server looking at the list, *point to the price* of a wine that's close to what you want to spend and then say, "We were looking at this one. What do you think?"
   - Keep pointing long enough for the server to see the price, and you'll be understood without having to say (in front of your date or client), "No more than thirty bucks, okay?"

I ask my waiters to point to the price, starting at a moderate level, with their first wine suggestion.

From there the guest's reaction shows his or her intentions, without the embarrassment of having to talk price.

There's no formula, but the bottom line is this: whether glass or bottle, it's hard to go wrong with popular grapes and styles, moderate prices, the "signature" or featured wine(s) of the restaurant, and/or the waiter's enthusiastic recommendation. If you don't like it, chalk it up to experience—the same could happen with a first-time food choice, right? Most of the time, experimentation pays off. So enjoy!

Wine List Decoder

Wine is like food—it's easy to choose from among the styles with which you're familiar. That's why wines like Pinot Grigio, Chardonnay, Chianti, and Merlot are such big sellers. But when navigating other parts of the list, namely less-common grape varieties and the classic European regional wines, I think many of us get lost pretty quickly. And yet these are major players in the wine world, without which buyers miss out on a whole array of delicious options, from classic to cutting edge.

This decoder gives you the tools you need to explore them. It reveals:

> *The grapes used* to make the classic wines—If it's a grape you've tried, then you'll have an idea of what the wine tastes like.
> *The body styles from light to full* of every major wine category—The waiters and wine students with whom I work always find this extremely helpful, because it breaks up the wine world into broad, logical categories that are easy to understand and similar to the way we classify other things. With food, for example, we have vegetables, meat, fish, and so on.
> *The taste profile,* in simple terms—The exact taste of any wine is subjective (I say apple, you say pear), but knowing how the tastes *compare* is a great tool to help you identify your preferred style.

The names are set up just as you might see them on a wine list, under the key country and region headings, and in each section they are arranged by body style from light to full. (For whites, Italy comes before

France in body style, overall. Their order is reversed for reds.) Finally, where applicable I've highlighted the major grapes in italics in the column on the left to help you quickly see just how widely used these grapes are and thus how much you already know about these heretofore mystifying wine names.

Sparkling Wines

- **Italy**

Asti Spumante	Muscat (Moscato)	Light; floral, hint of sweetness
Prosecco	Prosecco	Delicate; crisp, tangy, the wine used in Bellini cocktails

- **Spain**

Cava	Locals: Xarel-lo, Parellada, Macabeo plus Chardonnay	Light; crisp, refreshing

- **France**

Champagne	The red (yes!) grapes Pinot Noir and Pinot Meunier, plus Chardonnay	To me, all are heavenly, but check the style on the label: Blanc de Blancs—delicate and tangy Brut NV, vintage and luxury—range from soft and creamy to rich and toasty

White Wines

- **Germany**

Riesling	Riesling rules Germany's quality wine scene	Feather-light but flavor-packed: fruit salad in a glass

- **Italy**

Frascati	Trebbiano, Malvasia	As you've noticed, mostly local grapes are used in Italy's whites. But the style of all these is easy to remember: light, tangy, and refreshing. Pinot Grigio, the best known, is also more distinctive—pleasant pear and lemon flavors, tasty but not heavy. The less common Pinot Bianco is similar.
Soave	Garganega, Trebbiano	
Orvieto	Grechetto, Procanico, and many others	
Gavi	Cortese	
Vernaccia	Vernaccia	
Pinot Grigio		

- **France**
  - *Alsace—Grape names are on the label:*

	Pinot Blanc	Light; tangy, pleasant
Riesling	Riesling	Fuller than German Riesling but not heavy; citrus, apples, subtle but layered
	Pinot Gris	Smooth, richer texture; fruit compote flavors
	Gewurztraminer	Sweet spices, apricots, lychee fruit

  - *Loire Valley*

Vouvray	Chenin Blanc	Look for the style name: Sec—dry and tangy; Demi-sec—baked apple, hint of sweetness; Moelleux—honeyed dessert style

Sauvignon Blanc

Sancerre and Pouilly-Fume	Sauvignon Blanc	Light to medium; subtle fruit, racy acidity

  - *White Bordeaux*

Sauvignon Blanc & Semillon

Entre-Deux-Mers	Sauvignon Blanc and Semillon	Tangy, crisp, light
Graves Pessac-Leognan		Medium to full; ranging from creamy lemon-lime to lush fig flavors; pricey ones are usually oaky

  - *Burgundy White*

Chardonnay

Macon St.-Veran Pouilly-Fuisse	Every Chardonnay in the world is modeled on white French Burgundy	Light; refreshing, citrus-apple flavors
Chablis		Subtle, mineral, green apple
St. Aubin Meursault Puligny-Montrachet Chassagne-Montrachet Corton-Charlemagne		Medium; pear, dried apple, nutty; complexity ranging from simple to sublime

Red Wines

- **France**
  - ### *Red Burgundy*

Beaujolais Beaujolais-Villages	Gamay	Uncomplicated, light; fruity, pleasant

Beaujolais Cru:
  Morgon,
  Moulin-a-Vent, etc.
		More complex, plum-berry taste, smooth (the wines are named for their village)

Pinot Noir

Cote de Beaune Santenay Volnay Pommard Nuits-St.-Georges Vosne-Romanee Gevrey-Chambertin Clos de Vougeot, etc.	Pinot Noir	Ranging from light body, pretty cherry taste to extraordinary complexity: captivating spice, berry and earth scents, silky texture, berries and plums flavor

  - ### *Red Bordeaux*

Merlot

Pomerol St. Emilion	Merlot, plus Cabernet Franc and Cabernet Sauvignon	Medium to full; oaky-vanilla scent, plum flavor

Cabernet Sauvignon

Medoc Margaux Pauillac St-Estephe	Cabernet Sauvignon, plus Merlot, Cabernet Franc, and Petit Verdot	Full; chunky-velvety texture; cedar-spice-toasty scent; dark berry flavor

  - ### *Rhone Red*

Syrah, aka Shiraz

Cotes-du-Rhone	Mainly Grenache, Syrah, Cinsault, Mourvedre	Medium to full; juicy texture; spicy raspberry scent and taste
Cote-Rotie	Syrah, plus a splash of white Viognier	Full; brawny texture; peppery scent; plum and dark berry taste

Hermitage	Syrah, plus a touch of the white grapes Marsanne and Roussane	Similar to Cote-Rotie
Chateauneuf-du-Pape	Mainly Syrah, Grenache, Cinsault, Mourvedre	Full; exotic leathery-spicy scent; spiced fig and berry compote taste

(Red Zinfandel is here in the light-to-full body spectrum)

- **Spain**
  - *Rioja*

Rioja Crianza, Reserva and Gran Reserva	Tempranillo, plus Garnacha, aka Grenache, and other local grapes	Ranging from soft and smooth, juicy strawberry character (Crianza); to full, caramel-leather scent, spicy-dried fruit taste (Reserva and Gran Reserva)

  - *Ribera del Duero*

	Mostly Tempranillo	Full; mouth-filling texture; toasty-spice scent; anise and plum taste

  - *Priorat*

Sometimes Cabernet Sauvignon

Priorat	Varied blends may include Cabernet Sauvignon, Garnacha, and other local grapes	Full; gripping texture; meaty-leathery-fig scent; superconcentrated plum and dark berry taste

- **Italy**

  As you'll notice from the left column, Italy's classic regions mostly march to their own *bellissimo* beat.

  - *Veneto*

Valpolicella	Corvina plus other local grapes	Light; mouthwatering, tangy cherry taste and scent
Amarone della Valpolicella	Corvina; same vineyards as Valpolicella	Full; rich, velvety texture; toasted almond/prune scent; intense dark raisin and dried fig taste (think Fig Newtons)

- *Piedmont*

Dolcetto d'Alba (the best known of the Dolcettos, but others are good, too)	Dolcetto	Light; zesty, spicy, cranberry-sour cherry taste
Barbera d'Alba (look for Barbera d'Asti and others)	Barbera	Medium; licorice-spice-berry scent; earth and berry taste
Barolo Barbaresco	Nebbiolo	Full; "chewy" texture; exotic earth, licorice, tar scent; strawberry-spice taste

- *Tuscany*

Chianti/ Chianti Classico	Sangiovese	Ranges from light, easy, lip-smacking strawberry-spice character to intense, gripping texture; plum, licorice, and earth scent and taste
Vino Nobile di Monte-pulciano	Prugnolo (a type of Sangiovese)	Medium-to-full; velvety texture, earth-spice, stewed plum taste
Brunello di Montalcino	Brunello (a type of Sangiovese)	Very full; "chewy" in the mouth; powerful dark-fruit flavor

Sometimes Cabernet Sauvignon

"Super Tuscans"— not a region but an important category	Usually a blend of Sangiovese and Cabernet Sauvignon	Modeled to be a classy cross between French red Bordeaux and Italian Chianti; usually full, spicy, and intense, with deep plum and berry flavors

The bottom line on restaurant wine lists: In my opinion, it's not the size of the list that matters but rather the restaurant's effort to make enjoying wine as easy as possible for its guests. How? As always, it comes down to the basics:

Top Ten Tip-Offs You're in a Wine-Wise Restaurant

1. You're *never* made to feel you have to spend a lot to get something good.

2. Wine by the glass is taken as seriously as bottles, with a good range of styles and prices, listed prominently so you don't have to "hunt" to find them.

3. The wine list is presented automatically, so you don't have to ask for it (and wait while the waiter searches for a copy).

4. There are lots of quality bottle choices in the moderate price zone.

5. Wine service, whether glass or bottle, is helpful, speedy, and proficient.

6. Waiters draw your attention to "great values" rather than just the expensive stuff.

7. *Affordable* wine pairings are offered for the signature dishes—either on the menu or by servers.

8. You can ask for a taste before you choose a wine by the glass if you're not sure which you want.

9. It's no problem to split a glass, or get just a half-glass, of by-the-glass offerings. (Great for situations when you want only a little wine or want to try a range of different wines.)

10. There's no such thing as no-name "house white and red." (House-featured wines are fine, but they, and you, merit a name or grape and a region.)

Best Wine Bets for Every Occasion

Impress the Date—Hip Wines

White
Pacific Rim Riesling, USA/Germany
Frog's Leap Sauvignon Blanc, California
Monkey Bay Sauvignon Blanc, New Zealand
Lois Gruner-Veltliner, Austria
Kali-Hart Chardonnay, California

Red
Mark West Pinot Noir, Oregon
Joel Gott Zinfandel, California
Baron Philippe de Rothschild, Escudo Rojo Cabernet Blend, Chile
Catena Alta Malbec, Argentina
D'Arenberg The Footbolt Shiraz, Australia

Impress the Client—Blue Chip Wines

Sparkling/White
Taittinger Brut La Francaise Champagne, France
Matanzas Creek Sauvignon Blanc, California
Grgich Hills Chardonnay, California
Sonoma-Cutrer Russian River Ranches Chardonnay, California
Talbott (Robert) Sleepy Hollow Vineyard Chardonnay, California

Red
Etude Carneros Pinot Noir, California
Domaine Drouhin Willamette Valley Pinot Noir, Oregon
Duckhorn Napa Merlot, California
Ridge Lytton Springs (Zinfandel), California
BV Tapestry Reserve Cabernet blend, California
Heitz Cellars Napa Cabernet Sauvignon, California

You're Invited—Unimpeachable Bottles to Bring to Dinner

(You *do* still have to send a note the next day.)

White
Trimbach Riesling, Alsace, France
Robert Mondavi Napa Fume Blanc, California
Joseph Drouhin Pouilly-Fuisse, France
Chalk Hill Chardonnay, California

Red
Calera Central Coast Pinot Noir, California
Ruffino Chianti Classico Riserva Ducale Gold
　　Label, Italy
Penfolds Bin 389 Cabernet Sauvignon/Shiraz, Australia
St. Clement Napa Cabernet Sauvignon, California
Mt. Veeder Napa Cabernet Sauvignon, California

Wedding Wines—Affordable and Worthy of the Occasion

Ask the caterer or venue for these selections.

Sparkling
Aria Estate, Cava, Spain
Chandon Brut, California

White
Clos du Bois Pinot Grigio, California
Robert Mondavi Fume Blanc, California
Hess Select Chardonnay, California

Red
Robert Mondavi Private Selection Pinot Noir, California
Chateau Ste. Michelle Indian Wells Merlot, Washington
Souverain Cabernet Sauvignon, California

Affordable Agers

Like many wine geeks, my husband John and I especially like wines with bottle age. For certain wines, a little bottle age or even a lot brings in flavors that simply can't exist in a young wine. For reds, that's often flavors of leather and mushrooms; for whites it's often a nutty-toasty, caramelized flavor. For both, the overall wine becomes more subtle and more complex at the same time. For me, there's nothing like a great wine with the right amount of bottle age.

Like many parents, we want to buy some wine to commemorate the birth year of our children, to hopefully share with them when they reach the legal age. The problem is that the best-known wines for reliable aging are often very expensive. So to help solve that problem, we have put together our list of "affordable agers." Of course, what is "affordable" depends on the person, and since there are so few wines that age well below $20, we have come up with three ager categories:

> Affordable agers - Wines under $50 that age gracefully
>
> Splurge-worthy agers - Wines between $50 and $150 that age well
>
> The Big Guns - Elite, classic wines over $150 that age well, and typically appreciate in value, with age (Chateau Latour, Romanee-Conti, Araujo, etc.)

Below is a selection of the most broadly available bottles from this year's Top Ten wines. We taste aged wine as often as we can, and will update this section of the book every year.

Note that we have included some "agers" for medium-term cellaring, because we like to put bottles aside to mark annual milestones like anniversaries and birthdays. When appropriate I have indicated the number of years the wine will age gracefully if stored in reasonably cool cellar conditions.

Region	Affordable Agers*	Splurge-worthy Agers
Bordeaux red*		
Graves	Carbonnieux	Smith-Haut-Lafitte
Margaux	Lascombes, Angludet	Palmer, d'Issan
Pauillac	Clerc-Milon	Lynch-Bages
St. Julien	Lagrange, Leoville-Poyferre	Leoville-Barton
Ste. Estephe	Ormes de Pez	Calon-Segur
St. Emilion	Haut-Faugeres	Angelus, Canon
Rhone red	Alain Graillot Crozes-Hermitage	Guigal Cote-Rotie Brune et Blonde, Chapoutier Hermit-age
Burgundy Red (7-10 yr)	Nicolas Potel Savi-gny-Les-Beaune, Faiveley Mercurey	d'Angerville Vol-nay, Jadot Beaune Clos des Ursules
Burgundy White (5-7 yr)	M. Colin St. Aubin	Louis Latour Cor-ton-Charlemagne
California Cabernet Sauvignon	Mt. Veeder, Robert Mondavi Napa, St. Clement	Mondavi Reserve, Ridge Monte Bello, Grgich Hills Estate, Beringer Private Reserve, BV Georges de Latour
Pinot Noir (7-10 yr)	Etude, Lynmar	Williams-Selyem, Rochioli, Calera, Merry Edwards
Chardonnay (6-8 yr)	Chalk Hill, Chalone, Franciscan Cuvee Sauvage	Ramey, Staglin
Oregon Pinot Noir (7-10 yr)	Cristom, Sokol-Blosser	Domaine Drouhin Oregon
Italy (8-12 yr)	Frescobaldi Chianti Rufina Riserva	Solengo, Badia a Coltibuono Sangio-veto
Australia	Penfolds Bin 389 Cabernet-Shiraz & Kalimna Bin 28	Penfolds St. Henri Shiraz & Bin 707 Cabernet
Spain	La Rioja Alta Gran Reserva, Teofilo Reyes Ribera del Duero	Torre Muga Rioja, Marques de Mur-rieta Rioja

*The great chateaus of Bordeaux are an expensive category; as such we have defined "affordable" as under $100.

Cuisine Complements

Whether you're dining out, ordering in, or whipping it up yourself, the following wine recommendations will help you choose a wine to flatter the food in question. If your store doesn't carry that specific wine bottle, ask for a similar selection.

Thanksgiving Wines

More than any other meal, the traditional Thanksgiving lineup features a pretty far-flung range of flavors—from gooey-sweet yams to spicy stuffing to tangy cranberry sauce and everything in between. These wines are like a group hug for all the flavors at the table and the guests around it. My tip: choose a white and a red, put them on the table, and let the diners taste and help themselves to whichever they care to drink. (Selections are listed by body style—lightest to fullest.)

	White	Red
S T E A L	Cupcake Pinot Grigio, Italy Pacific Rim Riesling (USA/Germany) Kendall-Jackson Sauvignon Blanc, California Pierre Sparr Pinot Blanc, France Fetzer Gewurztraminer, California McWilliam's Hanwood Chardonnay, Australia	Duboeuf Beaujolais-Villages, France Falesco Vitiano, Italy Castle Rock Pinot Noir, California Chapoutier Cotes-du-Rhone, France El Coto Rioja, Spain Joel Gott Zinfandel, California Wolf Blass Yellow Label Shiraz, Australia
S P L U R G E	Bollini Pinot Grigio, Italy Trimbach Riesling, France Robert Mondavi To-Ka-Lon Reserve Fume Blanc, California Lopez de Heredia Rioja Blanco, Spain Mer Soleil Silver Chardonnay, California	Williams-Selyem Russian River Pinot Noir, California Domaine du Vieux Telegraphe Chateauneuf-du-Pape, France Penfolds Bin 389 Cabernet Sauvignon/Shiraz, Australia Catena Alta Malbec, Argentina

Barbecue

Bodegas Ochoa Rosado (rose), Spain
Dry Creek Fume Blanc, California
Jacob's Creek Shiraz/Cabernet, Australia
Jaboulet Parallele 45 Cotes-du-Rhone, France
Ravenswood Old Vines Lodi Zinfandel, California

Chinese Food

Saint M Riesling, Germany
Jolivet Sancerre, France
Setzer Gruner-Veltliner, Austria
Albert Boxler Muscat, France
Castle Rock Pinot Noir, California
7 Deadly Zins Zinfandel, California
Duboeuf (Georges) Beaujolais-Villages, France

Nuevo Latino (Cuban, Caribbean, South American)

Codorniu Cava Rose, Spain
Woodbridge Pinot Grigio, California
Martin Codax Albarino, Spain
Crios Torrontes, Argentina
Argento Malbec, Argentina
Casa Lapostolle Cuvee Alexandre Carmenere, Chile
Rancho Zabaco Zinfandel, California

Picnics (all screw-caps)

Hugel Pinot Gris Select, France
Crios Torrontes, Argentina
Bonny Doon Vin Gris Pink Wine, California
Kim Crawford Chardonnay, New Zealand
La Vieille Ferme Cote de Ventoux red, France
A to Z Pinot Noir, Oregon

Sushi

Moët & Chandon Brut Imperial Champagne, France
Eroica Riesling, Washington
Martin Codax Albarino, Spain
Silverado Sauvignon Blanc, California
Schloss Gobelsburg Gruner-Veltliner, Austria
Joseph Drouhin La Foret Bourgogne, France
Kali-Hart Chardonnay, California
Calera Central Coast Pinot Noir, California

Clambake/Lobster Bake
Chalk Hill Sauvignon Blanc, California
Frank Family Napa Chardonnay, California
Cambria Katherine's Vineyard Chardonnay, California
Miner Family Viognier, California
Erath Pinot Noir, Oregon

Mexican Food
Hugel Pinot Blanc, France
Veramonte Sauvignon Blanc, Chile
Heidi Schrock Vogelsang, Austria
Miner Family Sangiovese, California
Wente Syrah, California
Wolf-Blass Yellow Label Shiraz, Australia

Pizza
Falesco Vitiano, Italy
O. Fournier Urban Ribera del Duero, Spain
D'Arenberg The Footbolt Shiraz, Australia
Michele Chiarlo Barbera d'Asti Le Orme, Italy
Joel Gott Zinfandel, California

The Cheese Course
Frescobaldi Nipozzano Chianti Rufina Riserva, Italy
Penfolds Bin 389 Cabernet Sauvignon/Shiraz, Australia
Domaine du Vieux Telegraphe Chateauneuf-du-Pape, France
Baron de Ley Rioja Gran Reserva, Spain
Taurino Salice Salentino Rosso Riserva, Italy
Pesquera Ribera del Duero, Spain
Rosemount GSM (Grenache-Shiraz-Mourvedre), Australia
Grgich Hills Napa Zinfandel, California
Mt. Veeder Napa Cabernet Sauvignon, California
Chateau Ormes de Pez, Bordeaux, France
Val di Suga Brunello di Montalcino, Italy

Steak
Chalk Hill Chardonnay, California
Leeuwin Art Series Chardonnay, Australia
Miner Garys' Vineyard Pinot Noir, California
Ruffino Chianti Classico Riserva Ducale Gold Label, Italy
Marchesi di Gresy Barbaresco, Italy

Shafer Merlot, California

BV Rutherford Cabernet Sauvignon, California

Beringer Knights Valley Cabernet Sauvignon, California

Robert Mondavi Cabernet Sauvignon Reserve, California

Groth Napa Cabernet Sauvignon, California

Chappellet Signature Napa Cabernet Sauvignon, California

St. Clement Napa Cabernet Sauvignon, California

Martinelli Vellutini Ranch Zinfandel, California

Salad

Villa Sparina Gavi di Gavi, Italy

Hugel Pinot Blanc, France

Leitz Dragonstone Riesling, Germany

Louis Jadot Pouilly-Fuisse, France

Mark West Pinot Noir

Erath Pinot Noir, Oregon

Vegetarian

Qupe Marsanne, California

Kim Crawford Chardonnay, New Zealand

Au Bon Climat Santa Barbara Pinot Noir, California

Castello di Gabbiano Chianti Classico, Italy

Jaboulet Parallele 45 Cotes-du-Rhone, France

Val di Suga Rosso di Montalcino, Italy

Entertaining with Wine

In my experience, people stress a lot about the wine aspect of entertaining—what to choose, how much to buy, and serving savvy. *Relax*, because the wine part is easy. There's no prep involved other than popping the cork, and wine can really make a gathering memorable. Here are my top ten tips for pulling it off with ease.

1. Set your budget to fit the occasion, and your comfort zone. At large or casual gatherings, any wine in this book's "Values" top ten lists will do you proud. For a dinner party with a special menu or a guest of honor, it's nice to trade up a little, and theme your choices to the dishes on the menu.

2. Serve one white and one red (at least). Even if your party menu is geared to a particular wine style (e.g., a burger bash & red wine), offer the other color, too, for those guests who strongly prefer it.

3. Offer a unique aperitif. Champagne is the classic aperitif (pre-dinner pour, usually with hors d'oeuvres), but you don't have to go with something expensive. Prosecco and Spanish cava are worthy budget bubblies. Rose wines and lighter whites like Riesling and Pinot Grigio also make great aperitifs.

4. Serve white before red, light before heavy, dry before sweet. For both wine and food, the fullest and sweetest flavors get served last, so they don't overpower the lighter dishes and wines.

5. Open the wines ahead of time. As long as you re-cork and keep them cool, the wines will taste great and you won't have last-minute stress.

6. An all-purpose glass is fine. Unless you are having a serious wine gathering, you don't need lots of different wine glasses. A good-quality glass with an ample bowl and thin rim will showcase most wines nicely.

7. Give guests a printout of the wines. A printed menu with the wine names is a nice touch, so guests can remember the names of the wines they enjoyed.

8. Don't fill glasses to the top. Pros leave plenty of head space in the glass for swirling the wine, which enhances the aromas. Many good wine glasses are designed so that a 5-6 ounce standard pour reaches the widest part of the bowl. At cocktail parties and wine tastings I go with smaller pours of 2-3 ounces, so guests have the opportunity to try different tastes, and then pour more of what they like best.

9. Calculate how much wine you will need. Each standard (750 ml) wine bottle contains about five 5-ounce glasses of wine. For a dinner party plan on consumption of about 2-3 glasses per guest. Multiply that times the number of guests, then divide by 5 to determine the number of bottles needed. For a cocktail party where you are only serving wine, estimate consumption of 1 1/2 per glasses per guest for the first hour, and 1 glass per guest for each hour after that. Divide the total number of glasses you think your guests will drink by five to determine the number of bottles needed. If a full bar is available at the cocktail party, figure that one-third of your guests will drink wine and then make the above calculations. A good rule of thumb is to assume guests will consume 60% white wine, and 40% red. Always have water and other nonalcoholic drinks available, too. For a bubbly toast, buy one bottle for every eight guests.

10. Host the easiest wine tasting cocktail party ever. Serve one selection from each of the Big Six grapes paired with a simple appetizer (e.g., Riesling & egg rolls, Sauvignon Blanc and goat cheese, Chardonnay and popcorn, Pinot Noir and stuffed mushrooms, Cab/Merlot and pesto bruschetta, Syrah/Shiraz and barbecued ribs. Arrange the paired wines and appetizers next to each other, buffet style. Give each guest a wine glass and menu/note sheet, and let them enjoy tasting their way through the different combos It's a blast!

FOOD & WINE PAIRING BASICS

Whether you are a wary wine novice or a certified wine geek, "What wine should I drink with...?" is a constant question. Why? I think it is simply that those of us who enjoy wine love food even more. And we intuitively sense the possibilities to enhance what we're eating by pairing it with wine.

But a lot of people think that getting it "right" when it comes to pairing takes a big budget and a lot of wine knowledge. Far from it. Isn't it true that in Europe, the simplest of country lunches and bistro suppers, with wine, are often among the most memorable meals?

Back home, wine can transform your everyday dinners. Whether it's takeout, leftovers, or your best kitchen creation, you can just pour a glass of whatever wine you have handy and as long as it's one you like, you're bound to enjoy the match. That said, a well-chosen match can take the experience from nice, to knock-your-socks-off. To see for yourself, try some of my simple pairing pointers. They're a lot of fun and no hassle, so you won't need to wait for a special occasion to try them. In fact that's the whole point: everyday dinner *is* the occasion. Here's to making the most of it!

Pairing Basics

When I started as a sommelier, the pairing rule was "red wine with red meat, and white wine with fish." And in those days red wine meant Cabernet Sauvignon and Merlot, and white wine meant Chardonnay. "Meat" was beef, and fish was flounder or sole. Then along came...Malbec, and Shiraz, Pinot Noir, Riesling, Pinot Grigio...and a host of global grapes whose varied styles and flavors invited all kinds of new foods to the wine lover's table. Salmon and shrimp morphed from "special-occasion" to staple, pork and lamb gained new prominence, and exotic techniques and seasonings like stir frying, smoking, Asian accents, and southwestern salsas evolved into simply everyday fare. Since then I've had a ball playing matchmaker for all of these grapes and food flavors. And like any good couple, the best matches are based on either complement or contrast.

Complement simply means linking up common traits. For wine and food, that can mean matching body or flavors: if the wine and food are on a par, neither gets overpowered and the character of each can shine. For contrasting matches, pairing disparate flavors in the food and the wine can showcase the complexity of each. For example, a slightly sweet or tangy wine with a spicy-hot dish gives the palate a reprieve from the heat, priming your mouth for the next tasty forkful. A rich, creamy or buttery dish can find new balance and flavor complexity when paired with a crisp, tangy wine to cut through the heaviness and showcase the flavor layers. Here are some specific ways to put these ideas into practice.

Pairing Principles for White Wines...
When it comes to complementing matches, I focus on the body of the wine and the dish. Simply put, that means light-bodied whites with light-bodied dishes, and fuller-bodied whites with heavy or rich dishes. For example, the best wines for crisp salads are the light and crisp ones, particularly Pinot Grigio and Sauvignon Blanc. Richer salads such as Caesar or tuna fish call for a richer white like Chardonnay. In the same vein, lighter cheeses like goat and feta love a sparkling wine or Sauvignon Blanc. Heavier cheeses such as Parmigiano Reggiano or aged cheddar, match marvelously with a rich Chardonnay or Viognier. For seafood dishes think about the body of both the core fish or seafood, and the heaviness of the preparation. For example, lighter Asian stir-fry preparation I'd match a crisp white; with a cream sauce or buttery dish (like Shrimp Scampi), I'd go with a richer white. On that note, generally the tangy/gingery/sweet flavors of Asian-accented dishes are well-suited to white wines with vibrant acidity, and even a touch of sweetness (think Riesling, and Sauvignon Blancs from New Zealand). This point can illustrate

either complement (tangy dish with tangy wine) or contrast (spicy-hot dish with sweet wine). And what about meat with whites? As a sommelier I've even served big Chardonnays to my guests ordering steak, pork and game. Remember, no matter what the pairing rule book says, the most important rule of all is: drink what you like.

...and for Red Wines

For red wines, again body is the basis for complementing matches. For example, a big Napa Valley Cab or Italian Super Tuscan red stands up to a big steak or a rich cheese like Parmigiano Reggiano or Camembert, but a delicate Pinot Noir or Beaujolais (based on the Gamay grape) is better suited to lighter grilled salmon, pork or chicken, and to goat cheeses. Beyond body, it's fun to also explore some complementing flavor matches for red wines. For example, the peppery spice of an Aussie Shiraz is the perfect flavor compliment to spicy dishes like barbecue or steak au poivre. Earthy wines such as Italian Chianti, Spanish Rioja, or Oregon or French Pinot Noir wines, are a great complement to earthy dishes based on mushrooms, grains such as barley and polenta, or legumes like lentils and chickpeas.

For contrasting matches, both tangy and tannic qualities in red wine can cut through richness in food. For example, tangy Chianti with cheesy tortellini, or tannic red Bordeaux with richly-marbled steak or prime rib, are great matches. Herbal flavors such as basil pesto, or a rosemary crust for lamb, make a fabulous contrast with the rich blackberry compote fruit flavors of Californian, Chilean and Washington Cabernets and Merlots. And finally, the ultimate contrasting match for me is a big, fruity red wine such as California Syrah, with dark chocolate.

When you put these opposites together, they bring out the best in each other. And that's really the whole point of pairing wine and food anyway.

THE BENCHMARKS
OF WINE

These are the elite - the wines that "matter" to collectors, and to sommeliers in the finest restaurants. I believe they also matter "for everyone" because they are universally recognized as the quality and style leaders in their categories. While I included in my tasting notes a few favorites from this list that I had gotten the chance to try recently, for the most part even I can count the number of times I have tasted these wines on one hand. What makes them so special and expensive is typically a combination of both a like-no-other vineyard site, and a particularly skilled maker. As I said in the introduction, these are wines about which you can fantasize until your lottery ticket pays off. Or, do as some of my wine club members do: save up your money, and go in together with friends to split the cost of a rare bottle, and share the tasting experience.

Champagne/Sparkling—
    Bollinger RD Champagne
    Krug Clos de Mesnil Champagne
    Salon Champagne
    Roederer Cristal Champagne
    Veuve Clicquot La Grande Dame Champagne

Riesling—
    Trimbach Clos Ste. Hune

Sauvignon Blanc—
    Dagueneau Pouilly-Fume
    Chateau Haut-Brion Blanc
    Chateau Laville Haut-Brion
    Chateau Smith-Haut-Lafitte Blanc
    Domaine de Chevalier Blanc
    Gaja Alteni di Brassica Sauvignon
    Sanct Valentin Sauvignon Blanc
    Tement Sauvignon Blanc
    Vie de Romans Sauvignon Blanc

Chardonnay—
    Coche-Dury Meursault
    Dauvissat Chablis
    Domaine de la Romanee-Conti Le Montrachet
    Domaine Leflaive Puligny-Montrachet Pucelles
    Gaja Gaia & Rey Chardonnay
    Henri Germain Meursault
    Jermann Dreams

Chardonnay (continued)—
Montrachet Marquis de Laguiche
Kistler Chardonnay
Kongsgaard Chardonnay
Louis Latour Corton-Charlemagne
Marcassin Chardonnay
Patrick Javillier Meursault
Peter Michael Chardonnay
Ramey Chardonnay
Ramonet Le Montrachet & Meursault
Raveneau Chablis
Sauzet Batard-Montrachet
Staglin Family Vineyard Chardonnay

Other Whites—
Calera Mt. Harlan Viognier
Chateau Grillet (Viognier)
Clos de la Coulee de Serrant (Chenin Blanc)
Granges des Peres (Rhone varietals)
Guigal La Doriane Condrieu (Viognier)
Jermann Vintage Tunina (Italian blend)
Yves Cuilleron Condrieu (Viognier)

Pinot Noir—
Armand Rousseau red Burgundies (any)
Comte Armand Pommard
Comte de Vogue Musigny
Domaine de Courcel Pommard
Domaine de la Romanee-Conti red Burgundies (any)
Domaine Dujac Clos St. Denis & Bonnes-Mares
Domaine Roumier red Burgundies
Domaine Leroy red Burgundies (any)
Dugat Charmes-Chambertin
Faiveley Corton Clos des Corton
Joseph Roty Charmes-Chambertin
Kistler Pinot Noir
Kosta-Browne Pinot Noir
Marquis d'Angerville Volnays
Mongeard-Mugneret Clos de Vougeot
Ponsot Clos de la Roche
Roumier Bonnes Mares & Morey St. Denis
Williams-Selyem Pinot Noirs

Merlot/Cabernet Franc—
Castello di Ama L'Apparita
Chateau Ausone
Chateau Angelus
Chateau Canon
Chateau Cheval-Blanc
Chateau Clinet
Chateau Clos des Jacobins
Chateau Figeac
Chateau Gazin
Chateau La Conseillante

Chateau La Croix de Gay
Chateau La Fleur Petrus
Chateau Le Gay
Chateau L'Eglise-Clinet
Chateau Le Pin
Chateau L'Evangile
Chateau Pavie
Chateau Petrus
Chateau Troplong-Mondot
Chateau Trotanoy
Chateau Valandraud
Clos Fourtet
Falesco Montiano
Leonetti Cellar Merlot
Masseto
Pahlmeyer Merlot
Vieux Chateau Certan
Woodward Canyon Artist Series Merlot

Cabernet Sauvignon—

Abreu Madrona Ranch
Araujo Eisele Vineyard
Bond
Bryant Family
Chateau Beychevelle
Chateau Brane-Cantenac
Chateau Calon-Segur
Chateau Cantemerle
Chateau Cantenac-Brown
Chateau Ducru-Beaucaillou
Chateau Giscours
Chateau Haut-Brion
Chateau Lafite-Rothschild
Chateau La Mission-Haut-Brion
Chateau Latour
Chateau Leoville-Barton
Chateau Leoville-Las-Cases
Chateau Leoville-Poyferre
Chateau Montrose
Chateau Mouton-Rothschild
Chateau Palmer
Chateau Pichon-Longueville Comtesse de Lalande
Chateau Pichon-Longueville Baron
Chateau Pontet-Canet
Chateau Rausan-Segla
Chateau Talbot
Colgin Cellars
Clos Apalta
Dalla Valle
David Arthur
Delille Cellars
Gargiulo GMajor7
Grace Family Vineyard
Harlan Estate

Cabernet Sauvignon (continued)—

Heitz Martha's Vineyard
Hestan
Hundred Acre
Joseph Phelps Insignia
Karl Lawrence
La Mondotte
Leeuwin Estate Art Series
Leonetti Cellar
Lokoya
Nicolas Catena Zapata
Nickel & Nickel
Ornellaia
Penfolds Bin 707
Ridge Monte Bello
Sassicaia
Screaming Eagle
Shafer Hillside Select
Staglin Family Vineyard
Stag's Leap Wine Cellars Cask 23, SLV & Fay
Viader
Woodward Canyon Artist Series

Syrah/Shiraz/Rhone-style—

Chapoutier L'Ermitage
Chateau Fortia
Chateau Rayas
Chave Hermitage
Clarendon Hills Astralis
D'Arenberg The Dead Arm
Grange des Peres
Guigal Cote-Roties (La Mouline, La Landonne, La
    Turque)
Henschke Hill of Grace
Jaboulet Hermitage La Chapelle
Jim Barry The Armagh
Penfolds Grange

Italian Reds—

Tuscany
Biondi-Santi Brunello di Montalcino
Ca' Marcanda Brunello di Montalcino
Guado al Tasso
Solaia
Solengo
Tenuta Sette Ponti Oreno
Tignanello
Piedmont
Aldo Conterno Barolos
Domenico Clerico Barolos
Elio Altare Barolos
Gaja Barbarescos

Giacosa Barbarescos
Sandrone Barolos
Scavino Barolos
Vietti Barolos
Other
Arnaldo Caprai Sagrantino di Montefalco
Dal Forno Romano Amarone
Giuseppe Quintarelli Veneto reds

Spanish Reds—
Amancio Rioja
Clos de L'Obac Priorat
Clos Erasmus Priorat
Clos Mogador Priorat
Finca Allende Calvario Rioja
Finca El Bosque Rioja (Sierra Cantabria)
Mas de Masos Priorat
Muga Aro Rioja
Numanthia Toro
Pesquera Janus Ribera del Duero
Teofilo Reyes Ribera del Duero
Torres Mas La Plana
Vega Sicilia Ribera del Duero

Other Reds—
Turley Zinfandels
Sine Qua Non reds

Dessert Wines—
Beringer Nightingale Botrytis Semillon
Chateau d'Yquem
Dolce by Far Niente
Fonseca Vintage Port
Quinta do Noval Nacional Port
Taylor-Fladgate Vintage Port

THANKS TO . . .

My husband John Robinson, for his continued creativity in refining this book and my Web site to be the best, most helpful tools for the wine lover that they can possibly be, including thinking up the Top Ten.

Mark Lion and Troy Molander, for making this book, and the new Andreawine.com, look & work better than ever.

Julie Robertson for helping to pull it all together, with a fun sense of humor on the job.

Publishers Group West, Perseus Books, and the major book retailers, for believing in this book.

DEDICATED TO . . .

John and our amazing kids Lucas, Jesse and Jack, who are sweeter than the finest wine. Thank you for continuing to inspire me.

And in loving tribute to the memory of the missing from Windows on the World, where wine really was for everyone.

THANKS FOR USING MY
Wine Buying Guide.

I hope you're enjoying some great wines! If you have friends and family who also appreciate great wine, and you want more guides, go to my website www.andreawine.com for a 15% thank-you discount and other special offers. Just enter the promo code BG2011THX at checkout to receive the discount. Or join my wine course and get a free guide. Pretty cool!

I'm also on Twitter (@andreawine) and Facebook (facebook.com/AndreaRobinsonMS)

finally..

Available at
andreawine.com

...you only need one stem
to optimize your wines.

BREAK RESISTANT

DISHWASHER SAFE

BEAUTIFUL

EUROPEAN LEAD FREE CRYSTAL

HALF THE PRICE OF
SIMILAR QUALITY STEMS

THE
ONE

by Andrea Robinson

BE SURE TO VISIT ME AT MY WEBSITE

www.andreawine.com
where you can:

CHECK OUT DAILY TASTINGS

I post a new video every day. Check out the schedule, get the wine ahead of time and taste along with me.

SIGN UP FOR MY WINE COURSE

Join my fun and interactive video wine course. After watching and tasting along, you will be in the top 1% of people in the world in terms of knowing about wine.

FIND GREAT WINES

You can see the on-line version of this buying guide, constantly updated for new vintages and new discoveries.

FIND GREAT RECIPES AND PAIRINGS

And to go with those wines, check out some of my favorite quick and easy recipes.

FIND OUT WHERE TO GO

Check out my show Local Flavor, where I take you on the perfect foodie weekend in New York, Paris, Napa Valley and 18 other popular destinations. It's a tough job but someone has to do it.

The website is a lot of fun.
You can taste along and share your views!

See you there!